Nostalgic Walsall

Part of the
Memories
series

The Publishers would like to thank the following
companies for supporting the production of this book

Aulton & Butler Limited Saddletree Makers

Frank Baines Saddlery Company

Castle Packaging Limited

Freshway UK

Hydesville Tower School

Jabez Cliff & Company Limited

Kendrick Construction Group

Kirkpatrick Limited

J & E Sedgwick & Company Limited

William Sharp (Structural) Limited

South Staffordshire Water Plc

Stanley Bros Limited

R Taylor & Son (Orthopaedic) Limited

W Thacker & Sons Limited

Walsall College of Arts & Technology

West Midlands Co-operative Society Limited

HP Westwood Butchers

Whitehouse Cox & Company Limited

First published in Great Britain by True North Books Limited
Units 3 - 5 Heathfield Industrial Park
Elland West Yorkshire
HX5 9AE
Tel. 01422 377977
© Copyright: True North Books Limited 1999

ISBN 1 900463 18 0

Text, design and origination by True North Books Limited, Elland, West Yorkshire
Printed and bound by The Amadeus Press Limited, Huddersfield, West Yorkshire

Memories are made of this

Memories. We all have them; some good, some bad, but our memories of the place we grew up in are usually tucked away in a very special place in our minds. The best are usually connected with our childhood and youth, when we longed to be grown up and paid no attention to adults who told us to enjoy our youth, as these were the best years of our lives. We look back now and realise that they were right.

So many memories. And so many changes: one-way traffic systems, pedestrianisation, self-service shopping. How strange it felt at first to pick up a basket (those were the days before shopping trolleys!) and help ourselves from the goods on display on the shelves - it was almost like stealing! The trend led eventually to out-of-town shopping centres.

Through the bad times and the good, however, Walsall not only survived but prospered. We have only to compare the town as it is today with its new pedestrian precincts and shopping facilities with the town as it was, say in the 1940s, to see what progress has been realised and what achievements have been made over the last 50 years. Walsall has a history to be proud of - but more importantly, a great future to look forward to, into the new millennium and beyond.

Contents

Section one

Events & occasions

•

Section two

At leisure

•

Section three

Wartime

•

Section four

On the home front

•

Section five

Bird's eye view

Section six

On the move

Section seven

Shopping spree

•

Section eight

At work

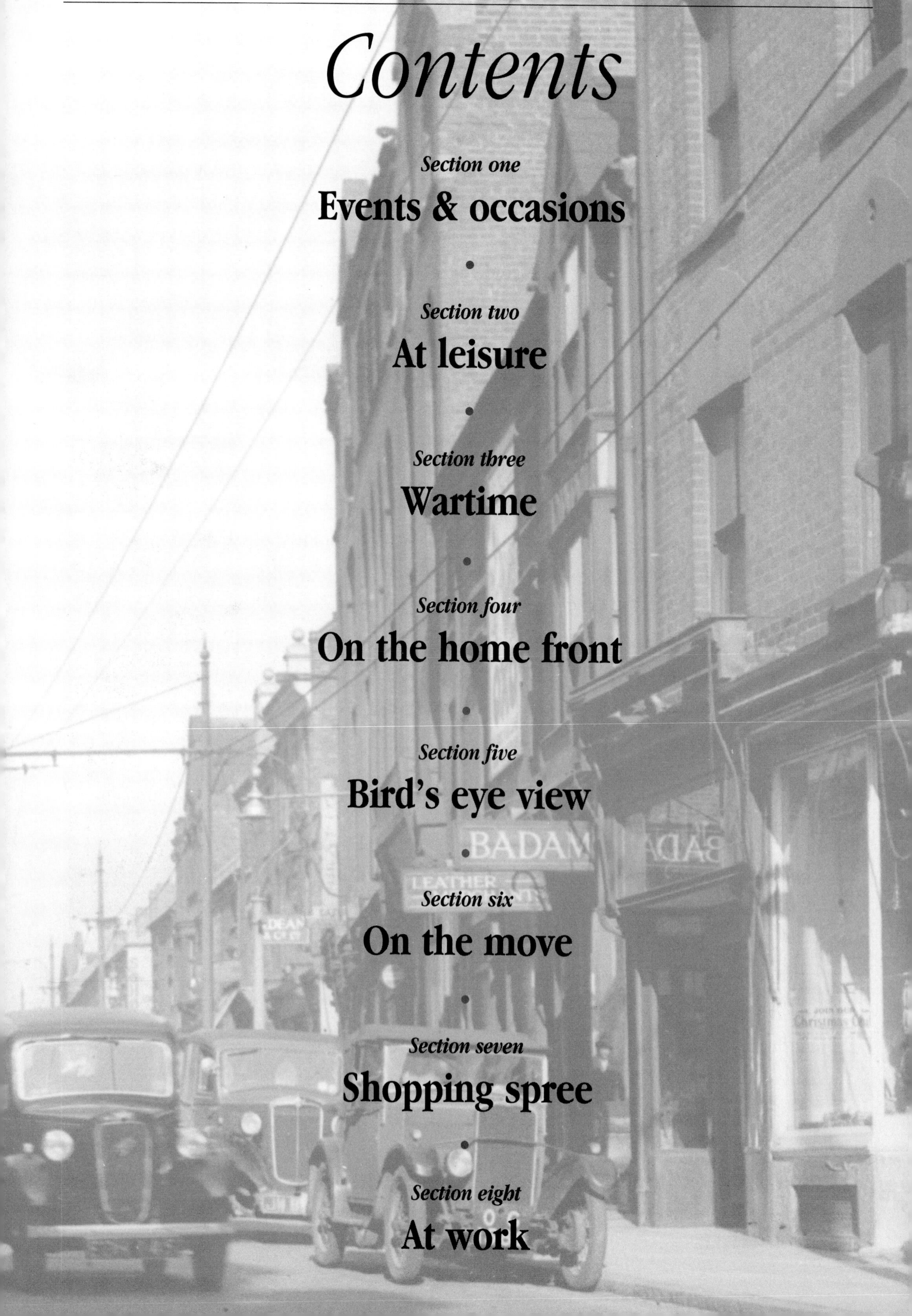

Events & occasions

This group of eminent citizens has gathered here to commemorate the construction of the five thousandth house built by Walsall Corporation under the housing acts. After the first world war the Government had made local councils responsible for the provision of housing, with the Housing Act of 1924 offering a financial incentive in the form of a payment to the Council for each house built. In the mid-30s this incentive was restricted to houses built under slum clearance schemes, in recognition of the health dangers now known to result from overcrowding. Mayor Gertrude Cresswell, seen on this photograph, did a great deal to improve social conditions in Walsall. A teacher and a Justice of the Peace, she was first elected Councillor in 1925 and became Walsall's first Lady Mayor in 1934. She was especially committed to working to improve child welfare and maternity provision. Indeed, she had good reason to be concerned over these issues; records from the first part of the 20th century show that for many years Walsall had the highest rate of infant mortality of any town in Britain.

The date was 30th August 1930 - the day of Walsall's big carnival. The carnival was a red letter day for local families, and the children in particular would have been eagerly looking forward to the event for weeks beforehand. Smiles of genuine happiness light up the faces of these young participants as they gaily wave their collecting tins for the photographer; the proceeds of the event were destined for the coffers of the hospital, and the eager girls in this photograph (perhaps they were off-duty nurses?) would have done a lot of box-rattling during the day as they passed among the good-natured crowds, expecting them to dig deep in their pockets and support this good cause. The carnival parade would have included marching bands playing foot-tapping music, and elaborately decorated floats. Hundreds of women and girls in the town would no doubt have been busy at their sewing machines for many weeks, running up the scores of different costumes needed. The theme of the costumes pictured here is not recorded, though perhaps the girls were meant to be clowns? The design of the trousers would have been unfortunate one, however, for any girl without the slenderest of hips and thighs....

Left: The war was over, and these Walsall factory workers were tired of bombs, gas masks, the blackout and all the other privations of wartime Britain. Out came the flags and the bunting and they strung them from pillar to pillar, turning their workshop into a marvellous riot of red, white and blue. When peace was declared after six long years of war a two-day holiday was given to workers, and along with the rest of Britain the people of Walsall went wild with joy. They might have been tired, but they still found the energy to let their hair down and organise street parties, dances and thanksgiving services. Huge crowds made a beeline for the Arboretum, which was kept open until midnight, and the occasion turned into a wonderful party. It was Britain's new Prime Minister, Clement Attlee, who brought the nation down from its euphoria with a resounding bump. He gave the country a serious warning that although Britain was once more at peace, there was no likelihood of prosperity for the country in the immediate future. It would be several more years before people could stop using tinned dried eggs or shop for clothes without counting how many coupons they had.

Above: Coronation Year, 1953, was a time for celebration. Wherever you looked there were flags, bunting and home-made decorations, and the shops were full of souvenirs. This particular shop with its special Coronation window display is Webster's papershop, at 15 Norton Road, Pelsall. Norton's could expect to do a good trade in items such as Coronation mugs, flags for the children to wave, and, after the event, printed souvenir booklets containing photographs of the whole magnificent procession. This shop is still a newsagent and still recognisable, though the frontage has been developed and it is no longer Webster's.

Bottom: This decorated float advertising Webster's paper shop was photographed at the Pelsall Carnival; however, the notice just above the numberplate reads '1951 Festival', so maybe Webster's used the same decking-out for the Festival of Britain celebrations and for the Carnival! Their banners are so effective that they certainly deserve to be used more than once, providing as they do very comprehensive advertising of Webster's services. Not only did they sell toys, sweets, books, comics, periodical and newspapers, they also ran a lending library for the convenience of the residents of Pelsall. And they promise to deliver your papers early - perhaps the boys on the float were out on their newsrounds early this morning before dressing up to advertise particular news areas such as Cricket News and Tennis News - long trousers seem to have been part of tennis attire. There is a banner advertising Roy Rogers too - do you remember the Singing Cowboy, alias the King of the Cowboys? You may remember that his horse was called Trigger, but do you remember his dog's name? Roy Rogers could be seen on ITV, valiantly upholding law and order, and was a popular character for many years. Oh, and by the way - his dog was called Bullet.

Below: What a marvellous occasion it must have been when these young ladies (and a few men) put on a Physical Fitness Display in Fellows Park. This particular dance involves several hundred participants, and as everyone who has ever attempted to synchronise the movements of a large number of people knows, getting an intricate dance exactly right is extremely difficult. Congratulations were obviously due to the choreographer who designed and organised the display! A sizeable crowd turned out that day to watch the event, and the costumes and hats of the ladies in the foreground bear out the suggestion that this photograph dates from the 1930s.

What a charming family scene - the smiling circle of bigger children holding hands as if to play Ring o' Ring o' Roses round the decorated street lamp with the little ones looking on and a well-dressed couple watching from the doorway. There is bunting across the street, too; the decoration could well be in celebration of the Coronation in 1937. We have not been able to identify the location, but certainly the houses seem very substantial, with decorative brickwork at first-floor level and ornate carved stonework above the doors and windows.

Above: This motley crew are the competitors in the fancy dress competition at Pelsall Carnival in 1958. Children never get tired of dressing up. The all-important decision of what to be, then the challenge of planning and making the costume - begging and borrowing accessories and enlisting help from any willing grown-up - is all just as much fun as actually parading on competition day. Some themes never lose their appeal: fairy queens, elves and pixies, Japanese boys in silks, Red Indians - here, one of them has a real pony. The Chef is more unusual, while the little chap to the right of the Red Indian's pony bears a placard which reads 'Pelsall Strong Miner', and very realistic he looks too, with a pit helmet, a dirty face and even a fag in his mouth. The box of Daz which is one of the other competitor's props, on the right, will come in handy for washing him clean after the competition. Mining, of course, played an important if sometimes tragic part in Pelsall's history. A monument in St Michael's churchyard commemorates the 22 victims of the Pelsall pit disaster on November 14th 1872. The oldest victim was 70, and the youngest was thirteen - not much older that the little lad in this photograph.

Above right: For it's Christmas all over the world, as the old song goes . . . Even without knowing the date or location of this photograph, we can see all we need to: the holly and mistletoe lovingly balanced on top of the

strip lights, the table laid with the fancy Chianti-style bottle of wine given pride of place, the rows of happy faces, and the squeeze-box player in the middle. It's a Christmas party, probably a works 'do' - the few men scattered around are severely outnumbered, and will have to be careful who is standing nearby when they walk beneath the mistletoe! It is possible that we are looking at a photograph taken near the end of the war; this would account for the lack of men to escort these lovely ladies home after the party. In times of greater prosperity, Christmas parties can be extravagant affairs with all kinds of entertainments laid on and more to eat and drink than is good for anybody, but surrounded by friends and with somebody there to strike up a tune, a merry time can be had by all.

From the youngest child to the oldest grandparent, the people of Walsall turned out in full force to watch the Civic Sunday Parade back in 1964. Smartly marching past in step are members of the British Legion; had the fathers and grandfathers of the small boys watching so solemnly on the right told them anything about the work of the British Legion, we wonder? It would be nice to think that they appreciated even a little of what the organisation was about.... During the first world war many servicemen returned home disabled; most faced an entire future of unemployment and the prospect of living on a pittance. In 1921 Field Marshall Haig formed the British Legion to present an answer to the problem; the Legion proved to be a powerful association whose caring force towards ex-servicemen and women extends to the present day. Their involvement includes providing emotional, financial and social support through residential and convalescent homes, visits to hospital patients and the housebound, holiday provision, Small Business advice, skill courses, employment - and even the provision of telephone alarm systems to people in need!

Below: It was 24th May 1962, and excitement was in the air in Walsall as this crowd of senior citizens awaited the passing of the Queen's limousine. It had been a long wait for these people; many of them had been so anxious to see the Queen in the flesh that they began to gather along the route of the procession some considerable time before the royal party was expected to arrive in the town - at least one of these elderly ladies had the foresight to bring with her a warm tartan rug to keep her warm. One young grandchild disconsolately clutching her union jack was obviously fed up with the long wait; we can all appreciate how utterly boring children find the chore of waiting around. The older folk had a different attitude, however. It was of great importance to them to obtain the best view possible of Her Majesty; if they were lucky they might receive a warm and friendly smile and that characteristic stately wave as she was driven by in her shining Rolls Royce, whose royal insignia proclaimed its illustrious occupant. No doubt when the waiting was over and the Queen's black limousine glided silently past her, this little girl cheered herself hoarse and waved her flag as enthusiastically as the rest of the crowd.

Left: The Queen was here, and the crowds who waited expectantly in Bloxwich Road were at last rewarded for their long wait. The Queen's visit on 24th May 1962 was a red letter day for Walsall; across the town flags and bunting fluttered gaily in the breeze, and banners proclaimed a wholehearted welcome to the royal visitor. While in Walsall she visited Crabtrees works, where the founder's son, Mr J Crabtree, presented Her Majesty with a distinctive piece of silverware to add to her collection. Her visit took in the Council House, where she signed the visitor's book in the Mayor's parlour; curiosity and a respect for the famous makes us wonder whose were the other illustrious signatures in the book!

Her Majesty's magnificent Rolls Royce Phantom with its distinctive rear glass canopy that gives onlookers a clear view of its occupant is a well-known sight to royal watchers; so many years on, the car is still in use today.

A number of readers will recognise Walsall's well-known author, John Petty, in the background of this photograph. He is the man on the right with the trilby hat and carrier bag. Mr Petty was the author of 'Five Fags a Day' and 'The Face'.

At leisure

Oh we do like to be beside the seaside! In the 1930s we never dreamed of going to Spain or Cyprus for our holidays; the seaside and a bucket and spade were enough. This young man has a very fine bucket indeed, with a Mickey Mouse scene painted all round it. He seems to be wearing a school cap, while the young lady on his left, judging by the blazer, attends Hillary Street Junior School - the badge appears to be the fleurs-de-lys of the Hillary Street uniform. However, on close inspection it looks suspiciously as though there is a button off the blazer, so perhaps it has been relegated to part of her play outfit, and either she will not be going back there next term, or she will have a new blazer to go in. Children's clothes in the 1930s were not, as they often are today, miniature replicas of adult fashions; they were happy to wear practically anything, cotton prints, rolled-up shorts, bits of school uniform, whatever make-do-and-mend clothes they were given, and these four are the living proof that, tousleheaded and happy, children can look charming no matter what they wear. But what we want to know is - what *have* they got in that bucket?

The happy couple and the wedding guests have gone off to the reception, and now comes the bit of the wedding ceremony that the children like best - gathering up the confetti that is left on the ground outside the church afterwards. This delightful photograph was taken outside St Matthews, and the enterprising little band seem to have a regular industry going; one of them even has a proper Confetti box to put the confetti back into. Which one was the ringleader, I wonder? The little boy on the left who is looking straight at the camera seems to be keeping a sharp eye on what is going on, so maybe he is the one who will decide when it is time for them all to to pack up here and go and play somewhere else on this lovely sunny day. In the 1930s, of course, it is likely that these children did not even have television sets at home, let alone computers to tempt them to stay indoors. So as long as one of the group was considered responsible enough to make sure they kept out of trouble, children were free to a large extent to play outside and make up their own games; in those days, parents had less cause to worry about the potential dangers of letting their infants out of sight.

Above: The installation of a slide at Reedswood Park in 1928 must have created great excitement, and no doubt when the lucky children on this picture go back to school on Monday morning they will not be able to resist saying to their classmates, 'Have you been on the slide yet? I have!' Whether or not the slide would pass today's much more exacting safety standards is another matter - we might be concerned about the rough mounds of concrete in which the slide's feet are anchored, and which might graze the kiddies' knees. But in the 1920s it was marvellous just to have a slide, and Walsall Corporation generously undertook one to install one like this in all its parks.

Below right: Freak Shows such as this were for a long time a perfectly acceptable, and indeed popular, part of the fair. This particular Fat Lady, who is lighting the dwarf's pipe with an oversize Bryant and May's British Made Special Safety Match, is Fatty Bayley, who worked for Pat Collins' fair. Pat Collins was a successful Midlands showman who toured round the area, putting in a regular appearance at the big fairs in King's Lynn, Nottingham and other places. Many

fairground attractions have come and gone over the years; what appeals to one generation may seem stale, boring or in poor taste to the next, and fairs have to be alert both to the changing tastes of their audiences and to competition from new forms of entertainment on offer elsewhere. For instance at the turn of the 20th century Bioscope Shows, or moving pictures, were popular, but once permanent cinemas became established the novelty value of the Bioscope was lost - at this point Pat Collins astutely opened a chain of permanent cinemas across the Midlands. He could also have claimed the unlikely distinction of being the first man to make a profit from the Channel Tunnel! One of his rides in the late 1880s was the 'Cross Channel Railway', a real steam engine pulling trucks round a track with a covered section, representing the Channel Tunnel, which - on a similar principle to the Ghost Train - was kept in complete darkness. This ride was, not surprisingly, very popular

with the young couples. It is amazing to think that people were already imagining a Channel Tunnel well over fifty years before the first test bores were drilled in 1959, and well over a hundred years before the rail link was finally opened in May, 1994.

Left: *No, these gorgeous creatures are not, in fact, the line-up for a bathing beauty competition - they are bathers come to try out the new open-air swimming pool at Reedswood Park. This was opened in 1931, and swimming costumes have become considerably more streamlined and much easier to wear since then, thanks the invention of elastic and lightweight, stretch fabrics, Do you remember the way the old woollen costumes used to fill up with water and become so soggy and heavy that they had a tendency to drag along behind you, so in order to protect your modesty you always had to check that your costume was still in place before you climbed out of the water? The man in the background wearing a full costume is playing safe; had he just been wearing shorts he would have been in danger of swimming right out of them. Swimming hats, too, have improved immeasurably - they used to be made of thick rubber, usually with a chin strap to hold the ear flaps down. Your hair got damp anyway; if your hat was very tight-fitting it would keep more water out, but it would also tear more hairs out by the roots when you took it off!*

Below: *A typically peaceful scene in the Arboretum: the Poplar Path, photographed here in 1963. Many generations of Walsall families have enjoyed spending Sunday afternoons in the Arboretum, while generations of courting couples have found it an ideal place for an evening stroll and generations of tired, harassed individuals of all ages have escaped here to relax, snatch a few hours' peace and quiet and watch the world go by. The Arboretum became Walsall's first public park after being taken over by the Corporation from the businessmen whose brainchild it had been, but who had not been able to turn it into a profitable venture. It was the Corporation, too, which was responsible for planting the fine trees, carefully selecting species which would do well here such as pines, chestnuts, limes, laburnums, purple beech, weeping birch and rhododendrons.*

During the second world war dances were held regularly in the Arboretum to help keep people's spirits up, and on a more practical note land was given over to provide 100 allotments where vegetables were grown in support of the 'Dig for Victory' campaign.

A fine sunny day, and the groundsmen at Walsall Football Club are admiring the new ATCO petrol mower and roller which they hope will keep their pitch in tip-top condition for the coming season. Although we have not been able to establish the date of this photograph, the style of the trousers and the use of braces to hold them up - sometimes assisted, as seems to be the case here, by a bit of string tied round the waist - suggests the 1950s. The late 1950s and early 60s were, as football fans will remember, an exciting time for Walsall FC; they began the decade in the lower half of the Third Division (South), sitting firmly at the bottom from 1951 to 1954, then they then moved up one rung in 1955 before continuing a steady upward trend. At the end of the 1958-59 season, with the old Division Three North and South reorganised into Divisions Three and Four, they ranked sixth in the new Division Four, the following year they topped Division Four, and they began the next decade poised ready to rise rapidly through Division Three and go straight up to Division Two. Without knowing the date of this photograph, one can only hazard a guess as to whether this meteoric rise was due to the purchase of the new mower, or whether it was the club's new prosperity which made its purchase possible.

> **THE LATE 1950s AND EARLY 60s WERE AN EXCITING TIME FOR WALSALL FC**

The pleasant background of trees and lupins is part of the gardens of Wednesbury Boys High School, but these particular boys are concentrating so hard on their game that they seem oblivious to their surroundings. It is 1937, the year in which Alexander Alekhine regained the world chess title from Dutchman Max Euve. Alexander Alekhine might be remembered as the man who, as a party-trick in 1925, played 28 simultaneous games of chess - blindfold. He earned himself a reputation as a ruthless individual, and although not universally liked he was considered by many to be the best chess player of the day. He became world champion in 1925 and apart from the two years between 1935 and 1937, when the newspapers attributed his failure to win the championship to his heavy drinking, he held the title up to his death in 1946, beginning a long spell of Russian domination of the game. It is entirely possible that these boys may have bought one of Alekhine's books in the hopes of picking up a few tips that would enhance their chances of being picked for the school chess team - a great honour, then as now.

Wartime

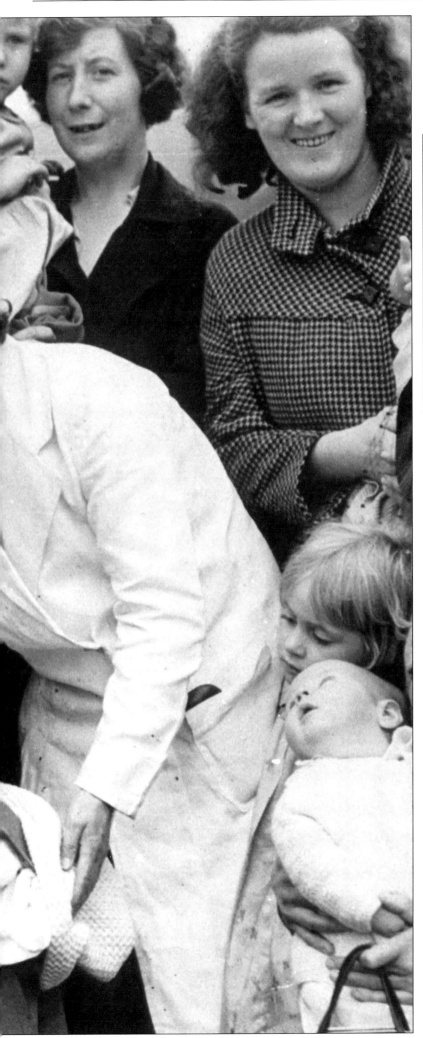

> **REGULAR GAS MASK DRILLS IN SCHOOLS ENSURED THAT YOUNGSTERS BECAME USED TO THE MASKS**

During the second world war babies under two were provided with special gas helmets, and special demonstrations were given to teach mothers how to use the potentially life-saving devices. Children were often frightened by the fearsome look of the gas masks, and the very young ones were given blue and red 'Mickey Mouse' masks, complete with ears. Regular gas mask drills in schools ensured that the youngsters quickly became used to the masks. When new, the rubber masks were stiff and uncomfortably tight, though as time went on they became more comfortable. Then along came an inspector who declared the mask unsafe and issued the child with a brand new tight and uncomfortable one.

The notice 'Hitler will send no warning - so always carry your gas mask' emphasised the threat of gas attack. Notices posted everywhere reminded people to carry their masks with them, though it was not compulsory under the law. Some cinemas and theatres, however, refused to admit people who did not have their masks with them.

Within a few months the fear of gas was receding and as people found that the cases made handy containers for make-up or sandwiches, the masks themselves were increasingly being left hanging on a peg behind the front door.

Bottom: It was embarkation time; goodbyes had been said to wives, sweethearts and sisters, who had no idea where their menfolk were bound for and would perhaps not see them again for many months - they tried to avoid thinking, 'if ever'. Walsall Station saw many such scenes during the second world war as men and women left to do their bit for king and country. Many of these soldiers wear a cheerful grin for the camera, but other faces betray a little uncertainty as to their fate; it is sobering to think that some of them might not have returned.

Right: This shiny new van was the generous gift of the Walsall Cooperative Society to the Air Raid Wardens Service during the second world war.
As early as 1937 local air raid precautions organisations were established in every district in the country, and air raid wardens appointed and trained. The Home Office prepared a booklet entitled 'The Protection of your Home against Air Raids' which was sent to every home in Britain. It encouraged every home and family to play an active part 'if this country were ever at war'. A section was provided inside the front cover for the head of the household to record the position of the nearest

wardens' post, the first aid post, and the name and address of their warden. At the beginning of the war, people who were prepared to work as ARP wardens were few, though the situation changed as war became a daily reality. Wardens were there first of all to give help and information. It was their job to patrol specified areas to make sure that no chinks of light broke the blackout restrictions. Constantly on the alert for gas attacks, air raids and unexploded bombs, they were responsible for the safety of local residents, and did much exceptional work during the war.

Gas attack was the big fear at the start of World War II; Germany had used gas during World War I, so they were fully expected to do so again. Even before the war began millions of gas masks were already being manufactured; factories up and down the country stopped manufacturing their usual products and were put to war work of many kinds, including the production of gas masks. The women in this wartime photograph are assembling gas masks for Walsall, though the subject was a bit of a sore point in the town, as older readers may remember. An incredible three months after the outbreak of war there were still people in Walsall who had not been issued with a gas mask. Even many of the children still lacked this piece of what might be life-saving equipment.

The threat of gas was a very real one; many veterans of the first world war suffered from the deadly, all pervasive mustard gas used by the enemy during World War I. So as soon as they got them the people of Walsall dutifully carried their gas masks every-where - at least at the outset.

Above: Thousands of sandbags were used during World War II to protect Walsall's hospitals, police stations and public buildings. Piled up outside doors and windows, sandbags provided excellent cover from bomb blast and prevented windows shattering, and the owners of shops, offices, pubs and on occasions even private houses also resorted to sandbagging their premises. Other people, such as the owner of this carpet and linoleum shop, stuck tape in criss-cross patterns across their windows or covered them with net to prevent injury from flying glass should there be an air raid. At the beginning of the war, trenches were dug in open places around the town which were later made into permanent shelters. Sir John Anderson, the Home Secretary, distributed around a million domestic air raid shelters coutrywide; made from corrugated iron and re-inforced cement they offered excellent protection from a direct or a near miss. In Walsall over a thousand Anderson shelters were sunk in private gardens; the shelters were free to families on a low income, though not everyone who wanted a shelter was provided with one. Many people preferred to retreat to the cubby-hole below their stairs, however, when the sirens went.

An intrepid volunteer was the 'patient' in this Civil Defence demonstration that was staged in Walsall in 1940. In case of enemy attack, it was important for ordinary people to have at least a basic knowledge of first-aid, and trained staff (note the helmets marked F.A.P. - First-Aid Post) provided them with the opportunity to learn what to do if anyone was hurt. How to treat gas contamination, stop bleeding, bandage a limb, treat burns and scalds, dress wounds and treat shock would all have been dealt with. Before war was declared a little book called 'The Protection of your Home against Air Raids' was sent to every home in Britain to alert the general public to the dangers, informing them of precautions such as preparing a refuge-room and making it gas proof, the importance of blackout curtains, what to do in the event of fire, and most importantly, first aid hints. A list of simple first aid supplies was given, and every home was advised to have lint, cotton wool, bandages and iodine on hand. The book's carefully-worded introduction began, 'If this country were ever at war....', though in some quarters there was little doubt that war was inevitable.

Bottom: Everyone loves a parade, especially if there is a rousing band to keep everyone in step. This photograph does not show a band, but these smartly turned-out troops marching past the Town Hall in perfect step almost certainly had one at their head. We cannot be certain of the occasion or the actual date of this photograph, but this march-past is very likely to have been a Victory Parade staged to celebrate the end of the second world war in 1945. Unfortunately the crowd is out of shot, but people would have gathered in their hundreds to welcome home the returning troops. During the war parades had become an accepted part of life; children loved the excitement of the rousing bands and the marching soldiers, and parades undoubtedly made the average person in the street feel in touch with the military and the progress of the war. When war was declared back in 1939 the people of Walsall along with the rest of the country had put their shoulders to the wheel and played their part for king and country. Now, they were simply glad that the long conflict was over at long last.

Right: Here is a sight to bring back memories - the Spitfire Walsall II, built during the second world war with money raised in the town, and photographed on 27th June 1941. In Walsall, as in virtually every town in Britain, a number of schemes operated to encourage people to join the war effort, and the citizens of Walsall did join in wholeheartedly. They dug for Victory in allotments in the Arboretum, and were very conscientious about saving their salvage and collecting for, and contributing to, National Savings campaigns. One scheme in particular has misleadingly modern overtones - people were asked to collect items made of aluminium to provide material for use in aircraft construction. The items they donated, though, tended to be 'tin baths' and other household items, not pop cans!

Around the town centre

The younger generation are obviously enjoying the flash flood that followed a heavy rainstorm, turning Park Street into 'Park Lake' on 14th June 1931 - though their parents, grandparents and more sensible older siblings huddle miserably in shop doorways and along the wall where the pavement underfoot is slightly dryer. Scenes such as this were common in the town centre, especially around Bridgeman Street and the railway station, and flooding was destined to continue to be a regular occurrence for many years to come. Eventually a new storm drain was installed to provide a solution to the age-old problem.

A sale was in progress at Boots 'Cash' Chemists,

REGULAR FLOODING OCCURRED IN THE TOWN CENTRE UNTIL A STORM DRAIN WAS INSTALLED

where no fewer than six lamps would have focused every passer-by's attention on their window display. We perhaps would have considered these displays as being rather dull compared with the windows of today's chemist's, that sparkle with jewellery, hair ornaments, cameras and cosmetics. Boots was the place to go, however, not only to have your doctor's medicines dispensed (note the sign 'National Health Insurance Dispensing') but to buy the popular home remedies that had stood the test of time: castor oil, ipecacuanha, camphorated oil, Indian Brandee and Fennings fever powders. Interestingly, the rooms above the shop appear to have been given over to the Boots Book Lover's Library.

Bottom: A view of Stafford Street that no longer exists today, as many of the old buildings in this photograph were destined for eventual demolition and development. Hewitt's well-stocked window on the far right is quite fascinating; pairs of boots hang not only in the window but outside it and in the doorway as well, reflecting the demand for such stout footwear in 1937.

Stafford Street is quite busy with traffic, with both private cars and public transport occupying the road (though it is blessedly free from yellow lines and parking restrictions!). Pedal power is obviously preferred by a couple of young men passing the cinema, while four-legged delivery is taking place on the left of the photograph. Horse-drawn vehicles continued to be widely used, particularly for delivery, through the 1940s and even in some cases into the 50s. The Stafford Street of 1937 carries a foretaste of the frenzied haste and hurry that was to characterise this same stretch of road in future years. A far cry from the days when noise from the town's traffic involved only the rattle of wheels and the trotting of hooves, and the only traffic pollution could be put to good use on the land!

Below: Between the two world wars a staggering 120,000 people were killed on British roads. The Minister of Transport, Leslie Hore Belisha, was concerned and called for new regulations. He introduced the first pedestrian crossings, and in 1934 the Road Traffic Act brought in the speed limit of 30mph in built up areas and made driving tests compulsory for new drivers.

Where did they all go to? Police officers on point duty, that is. There was a time when every major junction in every major town had its traffic 'bobby'; remember those black and white zebra-striped boxes they used to use? The boxes made them highly visible and gave them the elevation and air of authority they needed. Point duty must have demanded a high concentration of manpower, however, and it was no doubt argued that instead of directing the town's traffic the police force would be better employed in concentrating their efforts on the fight against crime. So a few at a time they departed, leaving the motorist with a legacy of traffic lights to contend with at each junction. Traffic lights, while no doubt keeping the traffic flowing smoothly through the town centre (in theory at least), somehow lack the personal touch provided by the good old British bobby. There appears to be little traffic to direct, but even so this particular bobby does not seem to have noticed the little boy about to take off across the road on his unusually-designed tricycle. The photograph was taken in Digbeth around 1950, and the spire of St Matthew's juts into the skyline.

A flock of sheep in the town centre would be a rare sight today, and younger readers might scratch their heads and ponder on the reason why these sheep should be bringing a line of traffic in Park Street to a total standstill. But apparently not only flocks of sheep but herds of cows were a common sight back in the 1930s, when this fascinating photograph was taken. The animals were brought into the town by rail and were unloaded at Walsall Railway Station's cattle dock in Station Street. From there they made the final part of what was to be their last journey under their own steam; their final destination was the abattoir in Short Acre Street. A vegetarian would have shuddered at the sight, but we must remember that in the 1930s vegetarians were few and far between, and people who believed in 'diet reform' were generally written off as being eccentric. It was to be many more years before the concept of vegetarianism was taken seriously, and campaigners such as the late Linda McCartney did much to make her beliefs accepted generally. Today, schools, hospitals, restaurants and airlines all make sure that their menus provide alternative meals for the non meat eater.

Right: Jaywalking was not so dangerous when buses and cars looked like this; the mother and daughter who are crossing the road and the man with his dog can afford take their time, without fear of being mown down by fast-accelerating traffic. The white stripes painted round the tree must indicate preparations for the blackout, which would place this photograph in the late 1930s. When the photographer took this snapshot he would been standing with his back to the George Hotel; stand on that spot now, and you will find yourself getting in the way of shoppers coming out of Tescos. In one sense time has moved on since the photograph was taken, but in another sense it has actually gone backwards. We are looking at the new bus station in St Paul's Street. However, as we go to press this site is once more a scene of redevelopment; the lower part of the building on the site which Ennals occupied for many years is today hidden behind scaffolding and sheeting, and scaffolding and construction work once more extend across the area where the bus stands can be seen in the picture. Of course, the Midland Bank, in that reassuring way that banks have, manages to remain exactly the same no matter how many bus stations come and go.

Bottom: This view of Bradford Street, taken in the 1950s, is not so very different today. The left-hand side of the street has been redeveloped, with the entrance to the Saddlers Centre's Bradford Mall just off the bottom left corner, but on the right hand side the only significant changes are in the proprietors of the shops and the roofline, where some of the embellishments have gone, and TV aerials are now much in evidence. The long-established Turf Tavern, just visible on the right, is now called the Tavern in the Town and has a different fascia board, but otherwise the exterior of the building has hardly changed. The names above the shops have changed, of course. On this photograph Gadsby's stands next to the entrance to the Arcade. Built around the turn of the 20th century, this Arcade, with its fine glazed ceilings and spectacular balcony with cast iron columns and iron balustrades, was Walsall's first indoor shopping centre, and during the second world war its cellars were apparently used as air raid shelters. It has survived well, in good decorative order and holding its own with the new shopping centres which have sprung up almost on its doorstep. In the distance are the familiar landmarks of the Council House turret rising above the dome of the Midland Bank.

Above: Sister Dora's impassive gaze ignores the public conveniences on either side of her to take in a busy scene on the Bridge in 1953, where an intriguing situation could be developing in the left corner of the photograph. Is the police officer tearing a strip off this man (who does seem to wear a rather sheepish air), or is the man perhaps merely asking directions? Crossing the road at the traffic lights in this pre-buggy era is a young mum pushing a pram of a design never seen today. The elegant semicircle in front of the elegant George Hotel is a hive of activity, with shoppers, parked cars and delivery vehicles. A Bird's Eye frozen food van and a lorry about to unload its delivery of barrels - presumably containing liquid refreshment for the hotel guests - are between them just about blocking up the road. Shopping along the crescent including Keys, whose signboard offers cycles and radios to the passing punters; Slendos is next door (wasn't that ladies' lingerie?). On the right, adjacent to the George Hotel's smart entrance, is Burton's menswear, who had at least one branch, and sometimes two or three, in every major town.

Right: Springtime in Willenhall, and it's a busy shopping day in the market place; can we detect blossom on the tree in front of the cinema? The fine and bright weather has made it perfect for getting out to look around the shops, and the young woman crossing the road appears to have a well-filled basket. Mothers, too, are out in full force, proudly pushing their babies in those wonderful but space-demanding coach-built prams. The date given for this photograph is 1954, and there is little traffic around apart from the van parked outside the premises of the gas service. It would be fascinating to take a closer look at the goods on offer in the window, though gas cookers, hobs, convector heaters and gas fires would be the obvious conclusion. Was this the era of the ubiquitous Cannon Gas Miser? Once coal fires started to go out of fashion and heating one's home by gas became the 'in' thing, the economical Gas Miser, more functional than beautiful, could at one time be seen in thousands of parlours up and down the country.

Bridge Street has to a large extent managed to escape the attention of the town planners. The carriageway has been narrowed, and the shops' occupants, of course, have changed, but the fine Tudor House building on the right has altered little since its construction in, as the inscription above the door tells us, AD 1926. Further along,

the Observer building remains unchanged externally as well; on this photograph the illuminated Christmas trees on the canopy tell us that it is Christmas time, and date is thought to be 1966/67. Thirty years or so earlier, the Observer offices had been down by the Bridge, next to the George Hotel. The white pub advertising Double Diamond

at the far end on the right is now the Black Swan; opposite, the Walsall Mutual Building Society, with its crown-like dome, has simply become the Cheltenham & Gloucester instead, while to the right, the long building, which at the time of writing houses Walsall County Court, is still the Co-operative Society offices on this photograph.

Although major developments have come very close to this spot, in the shape of the Old Square precinct (within yards of the Black Swan but just hidden from view) and the new Tesco (just off the picture to the right) nonetheless this contrives to be one view of Walsall which hasn't changed much in the last thirty years plus.

In the distance Overstrand Restaurant is just visible, while a little closer to the camera and slightly to the left, the George Hotel building is still standing. The former was not built until 1970 and the latter was pulled down in 1979, so our photograph must have been taken in the seventies. In the absence of any ladies' skirt lengths - always a good indication of the year - we can look at the cars along the kerb for clues: a car from the Austin 1100 stable, a Singer Vogue, a Triumph, almost hiding the little Fiat parked behind it, and a Morris Minor or Traveller, together with the Mini on the opposite side by Lloyds Bank, all suggest the early to mid-seventies. Although the scene in the distance is radically different today and Park Street is now paved and has seats for shoppers, the buildings in the foreground have changed little. Most of them have new occupants, though Lloyds Bank is still there; the timbered building to the left of Lloyds has lost its leaded windows, which have been filled in and covered over, but appears otherwise intact. Pedestrianisation and major alterations to the immediate surroundings have changed the character of the street, however; indeed, standing today at the spot where this picture was taken, we would have behind us not the imposing entrance to the railway station booking hall, as when this picture was taken, but the entrance to the Saddlers Centre.

Above: When this photograph was taken, Guildhall, hidden by trees, would still have been in use as the Magistrates Court. Now a restaurant, it bears an informative plaque on its wall which records for posterity the building's history and reminds us, among other things, that there has been a market here since 1220, and that many years ago 'the High Street was Walsall's only through route'. The Austin 1100-type car and the Hills van are demonstrating that up until the construction of the Old Square precinct and Overstrand Restaurant it was still possible to drive through Digbeth and along High Street - except on Market Day, of course, when the whole High Street stall area would be crowded with shoppers. But construction work is already well underway, with a site office at the bottom left of the picture and a builders' lorry parked in what

is now the stall area, while beyond it scaffolding is supporting the early stages of Overstrand Restaurant. This phase of the work was completed on 3rd November 1970. From this angle the name of the shoe shop to the left of the lorry is obscured by the jutting-out canopies but it is of course Dolcis, while on the opposite side of the road the scaffolding is almost hiding the name on Newmans self-service stores. Towards the top High Street on the right, the police CID department used to occupy a fine old building built as a music hall and now replaced by Sainsbury's. Opposite, a number of old buildings have fared better. The Green Dragon and the Guildhall have both been renovated, and the cafe is still there too; many shoppers will have fond memories of the original interior of this lovely old coffee shop.

Top: A bustling 1970s scene in King Street, Darlaston, before pedestrianisation - and what an unmissable offer for Darleston's bachelors: Sketchley's will clean men's suits or coats for 6s 11d (just under 35p) and replace missing buttons free! Perhaps this is what is attracting the attention of the gentleman in the light-coloured coat and the chap wheeling his bicycle the wrong way up this one-way street - or perhaps they are more interested in the passing soft-top Triumph Vitesse. On the right a child, wrapped up warm in a woolly hat and scarf, waits for its mother to finish chatting. Why was it that when we were children our mothers always had time, even on the wettest days, to stop and exchange gossip with their friends, but there was never time for us to stop and look at toys in the shop windows?

The distinctive building half-way down on the left with pedimented gables is one of the few still standing. This street looks very different today, so if you don't remember the scene you might find it very difficult to guess where this is. In fact it is King Street, Darlaston, before it was pedestrianised in the 1970s to become King Street Precinct. You could drive straight up it in those days, and the 'Waiting Limited' sign outside Burton's even allowed you to park on that side for a short while - very convenient when it was raining, as in this photograph. In spite of the weather, there are plenty of men and women out shopping, but there are indications that the shopkeepers might know changes are afoot - to the right of the photograph, the window beyond the pet-shop advertisement for Dog, Bird and Fish supplies appears to have

been boarded up and taken over by fly posters, while the half-obscured handwritten notice in the cut-price shop beyond, headed 'Special Notice to All Our Customers', may well be announcing an imminent change of premises. In the meanwhile this shop can hope to do a roaring trade with its offer cut-price cigs at up to 6d (two and a half new pence) off packets of twenty. Fly posters have been busy opposite, too; on the exposed wall where a building has been demolished a poster is canvassing support for Jack Robinson, the Labour candidate in Darlaston South Ward. Higher up and to the left of the poster, the remains of what used to be upstairs fireplace can be seen. For now, the space where the building used to be makes a handy parking spot for a flashy MGB GT - but the motorist's days in King Street are numbered.

Below: The shops must be shut, otherwise Digbeth would not have been looking so deserted, with not a shopping bag in sight. Maybe it is a Sunday afternoon or a summer's evening, and the few men who are out and about are on their way for a pint - Digbeth and the surrounding area has been well provided with pubs for many a century, and thirty years ago had a wider choice of drinking establishments than it has today. The majority of the buildings seen in this picture have gone, to make way for smaller purpose-built shop units; Ye Olde Woolpack, the mock-Tudor inn on the left, was demolished for the second time on 1st August 1966 - the first occasion had been nearly three-quarters of a century earlier, with the demolition of the original 15th century Woolpack and the construction of this 1892 replacement. Further down, lettering on the side of Harry Orton's shop proudly states 'Established 60 years', and indeed his pork butcher's shop had been in Digbeth, though not always on this site, since around the turn of the 20th century. The last shop in the row, Character Shoes, had before that been called 'Phillips character shoes', while Hawkins, prominent in a new building at the end, used to stand between Phillips shoe shop and Harry Orton. Hawkins' new building subsequently became an amusement centre. Today, with this area occupied by market stalls, it is difficult to visualise it as Walsall's main thoroughfare, as indeed it used to be.

This photograph was taken from the Observer buildings in Bridge Street, so the windows on the left can be identified as part of Tudor House; perhaps the ladder propped up against the building a little further down is an indication of a window-cleaner at work. Keeping the windows of all the three-storey buildings along Bridge Street clean is a major task in itself, made all the more so as traffic in the street becomes heavier. We are well-positioned here to carry out a quick census of the traffic travelling to and from the Bridge - a couple of lorries, four vans, a concrete mixer and ten private cars, including a Mercedes and a pair of Morris

Travellers who waiting side by side at the traffic lights - obviously a popular model in Walsall. The time is approaching when one-way traffic systems will be needed in Walsall. Other signs of the times in this picture include the nameboard opposite for the Mayfair Ballroom, and, looking more closely at the traffic, the self-adhesive demister panel stuck onto the back window of the Mini which is following the concrete mixer - do you remember how difficult it used to be to keep the car's back window clear of condensation on the inside and frost on the outside, before they invented heated rear windows?

On the home front

Above: This peaceful scene in Walsall Road, Heath End, Pelsall, was captured on film on Thursday, 5th December 1957 - a cool December, judging from the snow lingering on the steps on to the left of the picture. A pint of milk on the doorstep opposite suggests that it is early in the morning. How different life was, forty years ago! Perhaps the man on the left is going to work, beginning his day with a brisk walk, with cap, gloves and a good thick coat to keep out the cold - very different from many people's morning routine these days, which consists of diving out of the house and into the car, and sitting impatiently in traffic for half an hour or so. Motor transport was less of a mixed blessing in 1957 - it had yet to take over our lives and become a problem in itself, but it was there when it was needed, for instance in the form of the ambulance coming down Walsall Road, with a little bell on the front. It is not just the big things that have changed - new housing has changed this spot beyond recognition - but the little things too; the pint of milk, for instance, will be straight from the cow, whereas today many families buy cartons of semi-skimmed, to reduce their fat intake; and to the right of the ambulance the little corner shop unrepentantly displays a Players Please sign, another example of how blissfully ignorant we were about our health. The people who live in these houses will rely on the corner shop and the off-licence opposite - there were no supermarkets in 1957 to offer a huge range of goods, but a good shopkeeper got to know what his customers wanted and kept it in for them.

Below: This lady walking in St Paul's Street looks unconcerned as her image is captured for posterity by a photographer. Not so the small boy behind her, who is as thrilled to have his photograph taken as were those people who waved frantically at the cameraman in the earlier years of television. The photograph dates from 1937, when only the more affluent families were likely to own a camera; having one's photograph taken was still quite a rare event. Looking towards Stafford Street, Richmond's furnishings can be seen in the background, with its sun blinds down. Of particular interest is the wall behind the group of children at play on the left, where a group of half a dozen posters advertise various newspapers and periodicals. The headline 'Marconi and messages from Mars' is particularly intriguing. It was 1901 when Marconi succeeded in sending the first radio signals across the Atlantic - and in 30 years radio had come a long way. We have no way of knowing what this fascinating headline about messages from Mars was all about, though a few years earlier in 1931 radio interference from the Milky Way had been discovered.

The bulldozers have been busy, and the transformation of the former Pheasey Farm land into Pheasey Estate is well underway. This rural site was purchased from farmer George Smith by the First National Housing Trust in 1935. The First National Housing Trust was a private venture, established as a subsidiary of Henry Boot, and its aim was to provide badly-needed housing for working people; the Trust had already undertaken similar developments in other areas, building estates of new houses, usually semi-detached or in blocks of four or six, and then renting them out to families. All applicants were vetted, and only those who met the Trust's criteria were either offered houses or placed on waiting listing list, to ensure that when housing did become available it went to the most deserving families. The Trust was deluged by applications for housing in the Birmingham area, and as there seemed to be no possi-

bility of finding a site in the City for another large-scale development, plans were drawn up to turn the 303,203 acres of land at Pheasey Farm into an estate comprising 4,225 houses with a school at each end and shops, cinema and a community centre, all linked by nine and a half miles of internal roads. Planning permission was refused at first as Aldridge UDC felt that the density of housing was excessive, especially in an area they had hoped to keep as 'green belt'. However, after further discussion it was agreed that the scheme should ahead, with the Council purchasing 68 acres to be preserved as an open space. On 13th July 1937 the Minister of Health, Sir Kingsley Wood, ceremonially cut the first sod using a chromium-plated spade. This photograph was taken in the late 1930s, and for many lucky Birmingham families the long wait for decent, affordable housing is over at last.

Bird's eye view

The top of the Cenotaph, visible slightly to the right of centre at the bottom edge of this photograph, places us in Bradford Street, and if we look along to the Bridge we can see two trams in the centre of the carriageway. To the right we can pick out the square, pillared George Hotel, built by Thomas Fletcher in 1781 and replaced in the 1920s by the building with the curved facade seen in more modern photographs; in fact, it looks suspiciously as if demolition work may in fact commenced here behind a screen at the far end of the building. The statue of Sister Dora seen here is the original marble version, subsequently replaced by a bronze cast made in 1956. Following the line of High Street to the right, the old Woolpack Inn, demolished in 1966, is on the far right edge of the picture, while about half way along High Street the Talbot Hotel can be identified by the lettering which runs across the white frontage above the first floor windows. Looking the other way from the Bridge into St Paul's Street, St Paul's Church is clearly visible. This church was rebuilt at the end of the 19th century, and in recent years has become a multi-functional centre including shops, restaurants and conference facilities. Facing St Paul's, on the spot which is now the bus station, we can see the Bluecoat School which moved to this location from its earlier site by the George Hotel on the Bridge, and remained here until 1934.

Industrial and residential chimneys intermingle companionably as we spy down on the roof-tops of Wolverhampton Street. In the roadway are a couple of motor lorries and a few clusters of people, although by today's standards it seems deserted. To the right, however, there is plenty of activity on the Cut - on the short stretch visible in the photograph a dozen or so barges are moored and piles of goods either waiting to be loaded or recently offloaded are stacked by the quayside in the lower half of the picture, while a couple of trucks seem busy by the canalside and there appears to be a hand-barrow by one of the outbuildings. In amongst the industry, domestic life goes on and a number of families have the washing out; just to the left of the warehouse with the undulating roof we can sneak a good look at sheets, shirts and other items hanging on the line. It is fortunate that the dense smoke from the industrial chimney, further from the camera to the right, is blowing in the other direction, otherwise housewives' tempers would certainly have become frayed! Defective rooves cannot be hidden from the spying eye of the aerial photographer either - one building has lost its roof completely and several others, including the building just left of centre on the bottom edge of the picture, are in a poor state of repair.

The cluster of trees just right of centre draw the eye, appropriately enough, to the Walsall's seat of government, the Municipal buildings on Lichfield Street. The foundation stone was laid on 29 May 1902 and the Town Council moved here from the Guildhall in 1905. A glance at the road layout on this aerial view shows the routes that existed through Walsall before pedestrian zones and one-way traffic systems came into play; a well-defined line runs roughly north to south along Lichfield Street and Bradford Street, crossed by an apparently equally simple east-west passage through High Street and along Park Street. Pedestrian zones and one-way systems have complicated matters for today's motorist, but in fact High Street was the main thoroughfare for many centuries, and Bradford Street was given to the people of Walsall by the Earl of Bradford in 1831 to provide a route from the centre of Walsall to Birmingham via Wednesbury and West Bromwich. If we look to the right of Bradford Street almost on a level with the zebra crossing, it is just possible to pick out dome of the Arcade and trace the line of its glazed roof. The inspiration for this fine Arcade came from local leather manufacturer and MP Sir E T Holden, more than a century ago.

Many familiar landmarks can be picked out on this aerial view of Walsall. We can make a brief circular tour, beginning on the left where we can easily spot the Cenotaph, dedicated on 1st October 1921 to the memory of those who gave their lives in the first world war. From Bradford Place we move clockwise over the railway tracks which terminate in the station building demolished in 1979, appearing strangely semicircular from the air. Emerging from the station and continuing clockwise over Park Street, we cross the far end of the old Bus Station, with its bays running north-east to south-west. A left turn along St Paul's Street takes us on a tour of the Technical College site, and we can then sweep round across the railway line, Hatherton Street and Lower Forster Street into Lichfield Street, where the tower of Council House shows up dark against the buildings beyond. Head along Lichfield Street towards the town centre, where a very sharp pair of eyes might pick out the outline of the clock which now stands atop the entrance to Old Square shopping centre - look for the unusually-shaped white block. Returning as the crow flies from here back the Cenotaph, we pass directly over another distinctively-shaped building, the old George Hotel by the Bridge, easily recognisable by its curved facade. From this altitude Sister Dora's statue is little more than a black dot.

Blessing or curse, here it comes - the M6 has reached Walsall! The entry and exit sliproads which we can see in the distance towards the top of the picture will lead up to the elevated roundabout junction with Wolverhampton Road at Junction 10; today, the Black Country Route off to the West provides a swift link between this point and Wolverhampton.

The outline of the motorway can be clearly seen running north of Darlaston Road, which crosses the picture horizontally just above the gasometers, and already the line which it will follow to the south can be picked out, although carriageway construction has yet to begin on this section. An overbridge will carry the motorway over the railway line running east near the bottom right corner of the picture, while the railway track which can be seen cutting across the left hand corner will continue to run south alongside the motorway to Tame Bridge and beyond. (It is now crossed by the M5 in the vicinity of Junction 8.) The entire length of motorway seen under construction in this photograph was open to traffic by the end of 1970, contributing to the 750 miles of motorway in Britain around that time.

On the move

The poster by the gate to the memorial gardens is inviting us to a Masque and Fancy Dress Ball to be held at the 'Town Hall' as part of The Mount Carnival - just what we need to cheer us up, on this rather grey winter's day with the trees still bare of leaves. The Pleck Dodger and the Number 38 to Darlaston via Wednesbury seem to have plenty of passengers but are in no hurry to depart, and an air of languid, post-Christmas inactivity seems to be hanging over Bradford Place. No doubt inside the College things are different

A SLOW EXPOSURE CAMERA WOULD CAPTURE A FAST MOVING OBJECT AS A BLURRED, GHOSTLY IMAGE

and the students are working away with a will, as students always do! It must be many years since a horse stopped to drink from the trough behind the lamp-post; and have you spotted the ghost cyclist overtaking the car immediately behind the Walsall Wood Colliery truck? This effect used to occur quite frequently when a slow-exposure photograph captured a fast-moving object, resulting in a blurred, ghostly image - quite appropriate for a murky scene such as this!

Above: Sutton Road and Birmingham Road Bus Station was the scene of a fair amount of activity when this photograph was taken back in 1930; buses are being boarded for a homeward journey, and one or two people appear to be intending to use this wonderful old 'Tardis' type telephone box without a thought that they might risk travelling through time and space to meet Dr Who....

Buses have long presented advertisers with an ideal opportunity to publicise their products, and these two mobile hoardings - the Number 13 and the Number 26 - are advertising Allsopps Milk Stout and Typhoo tea. Did any hapless passer-by ever try drinking Typhoo tea as a cure for their indigestion, we have to wonder? And did any of the sufferers get around to asking their doctor about its benefits? Perhaps there may have been some truth in the claim, given the lift that the caffeine would have provided. Be that as it may, advertisers at that time, we suspect, were not required by law to have the same regard for the truth as their modern counter-parts. By the 1970s Typhoo had changed their approach to the less contentious 'Join the Tea Set' and 'Typhoo puts the "T" in Britain'.

Right: During the second world war, with a large proportion of the male population away on active service, women had to learn to do a number of jobs which had previously been looked upon as 'man's work'. Life had to go on, industry had to go on, and somebody had to take do the work; there was simply no room for scruples over whether or not it was proper work for women. Suddenly, of necessity, the traditional male and female roles went out of the window, and attitudes were forced to change, although some men found it hard to come to terms with women literally wearing the trousers, genuinely thinking that the weaker sex would not have the strength or ability to perform heavy factory duties - or drive buses. Nora Thomas, Walsall's first lady trolley bus driver to complete training during World War II, may well have had to turn a deaf ear to a few disparaging remarks from men who did not have much confidence in reaching their destination with a woman at the wheel. In fact, Nora looks extremely capable and very smart in her bus driver's uniform. Her double-breasted coat and remarkably sturdy gauntlets suggest that the cab of a trolley-bus could be a cold, draughty place on a bitter winter's day. Certainly she was a very coura-geous lady; it comes as no surprise to see women driving buses and lorries these days, but we must not forget that the vehicles she drove were very different from the well-heated, power-assisted, hi-tech buses of today, and were more demanding in terms of physical strength and endurance. And driving round Walsall in the blackout must have been quite a challenge too!

Both pictures: Trolleybus number 862 went down in history as Walsall's last trolleybus. Here it is seen picking up passengers on the fateful day which saw the abolition of trolleybuses in Walsall. **Inset:** Buses, from the point of view of the West Midlands Transport Executive who took over the service from Walsall Corporation Transport on 1st October 1969, offered a number of advantages: there was no overhead power cable network to maintain, which made the service cheaper to operate, and from a planning point of view there was infinitely more flexibility when it came to changing the routes along which the service operated. On the other hand, there was the initial expense of buying the buses, and for a while it was necessary to borrow buses from Birmingham, so for a while Birmingham buses were a common sight in the bus station and in the streets of Walsall.

The driver of the trolleybus is Billy Moore, and the bus is seen on the left preparing to depart from North Walsall depot. People of all ages have come out to say farewell to this popular form of transport; the younger ones in this photograph will have grown up with trolleybuses and will not

Both pictures: Waiting for life to begin - Walsall's brand new bus station in 1935 was so very new that

building work was still taking place on one of the stands in the background. The new bus station was a much needed addition to Walsall's facilities, and was eventually to be greatly appreciated by travellers.

The bus station's site adjacent to St Paul's church had once been the home of the Bluecoat School which relocated to Abelwell Street, Birmingham Road. Most of the signs in the photograph are obviously for the general public; the 'Keep Left' signs on the right of the picture, however, are for the bus drivers' benefit, and would appear to Millennium drivers to be rather unnecessary. We need to remember, however, that those were the days when road markings were by and large restricted to white

lines painted down the centre of the road, while boards were erected to give instructions and directions to motorists. On platforms two, three and four, spanking new signs inform the public about which buses run from this particular platform. An interesting notice on Number 4 Platform says, 'To Parking Place'. Have you ever stopped to compare the road signs of earlier days with those of today? Old photographs such as these remind us that signs were at one time far more wordy than they are now: 'Halt at Major Road Ahead' was replaced by 'Give Way' or 'Stop'. 'To Parking Place' would today be simply an arrow with a white letter 'P' on a blue background. The new bus station eventually grew old and in 1970 it was redesigned, and the platforms built cross-ways. In 1998 it was demolished and is at present in the process of rebuilding.

Shopping spree

How different this looks today! In fact, Sister Dora is still there, the market stalls are still there and Bridge Street to the left is much the same; but what makes all the difference is that the George Hotel which dominates the picture has disappeared without a trace, replaced by a modern brick block occupied principally by Tesco to the left and going round the corner into Bridge Street, with the Halifax Building Society on the right and sundry shops, offices and agencies in between. The public conveniences, opened in 1912, have also gone, but Sister Dora is still here; this statue is a

THE GEORGE HOTEL, WHICH COMPLETELY DOMINATES THIS PICTURE, HAS NOW DISAPPEARED WITHOUT TRACE

bronze cast of the original marble statue which was erected in 1886 to the memory of Dorothy Wyndlow Pattison, who died in 1878, having devoted many years of her life to improving the medical facilities available to the working people of Walsall. Her death was mourned by thousands, and she became the first woman in this country, other than a member of the royal family, to have a statue erected in her memory. Exposure to the weather caused the marble to deteriorate, however, and this bronze cast was made in 1956 to perpetuate her memory.

The clock reads 10.25, and the morning's shopping is in progress in Willenhall market place; a number of ladies (interestingly, virtually all of them older ladies) are browsing among the shops, deciding, no doubt, what to cook for their husbands' meal that day. The photograph was taken in 1948; those were the days when women were not career-orientated. Their job was to bring up the family, do the shopping, cleaning, cooking and sewing - and generally keep their husbands happy. Housework, of course, was far more of a chore back then without the multitude of state-of-the-art gadgets to help them get through it quickly.

Perhaps older readers will remember shopping at the Bargain Shoe Warehouse on the right - and younger ones will realise that bargain stores are not a modern invention! Next door was the Talbot Hotel, where a pointing finger directs punters to the bar and smoke room. Behind the Clock Tower island was Henly's, with George Briscoe's grocery store next door along. Adverts in the window reveal that among the products sold there were Saxa Salt and Bisto gravy browning. Lovers of trivia will enjoy finding out that the name 'Bisto' is an arrangement of the initial letters of their slogan 'Browns, Seasons, Thickens In One.'

Left: It's Springtime, and the nice weather has certainly brought the market shoppers out in full force. High Street is a scene of bustling activity. Regardless of the changes that have already taken place, are in progress or are still in the planning stage for the surrounding area, a busy market can conjure up a very special atmosphere all its own. The derelict area at the top of High Street where Sainsbury's now stands makes a very handy parking place for the storeholders' vans, although it does nothing to improve the elegance of our view. This photograph was of course taken from St Matthew's Church, probably in 1979 or there-abouts, and at that time the renovation of St Matthew's was another subject of much discussion locally. From this angle the gradient of High Street is emphasised, and we have a clear view right across town, with the chimneys of the surrounding factories rising up against the horizon.

Below: A pair of white flares worn by the young man who has just walked past the Home and Colonial helps us to date this photograph to the early 1970s, and the passing traffic adds its own touch of nostalgia. The names Ford and Austin dominate the scene: the Ford Anglia estate in the foreground was quite rare, even in its day, and travelling in the same direction further along Bradford Street are a popular Austin Cambridge (designed by Farina) and a Mk2 Ford Cortina. Travelling towards us is an Austin, either 1100 or 1300, and a Mk1 Ford Anglia. Readers who are motorists may recall owning one of these fine vehicles at one time! The shops, too, stir many memories: the Home and Colonial, who had a chain of popular grocery and greengrocery stores; Halfords, who at one time concentrated more on cycles and accessories than on motoring; Peter Lord, and Hepworths. Above them, the upper floor was given over to the Curtis Warehouse. British Home Stores is in the background. The pedestrian crossing is worth a mention; note the unfamiliar sign above the lights in the middle of the road: 'To cross press button and wait'.

Above: The name 'Digbeth' means 'the dyke path', and the dyke in question would have referred to the now-culverted watercourse which runs under the bridge. This photograph shows Digbeth as it was in 1964, and if plans were being hatched to redevelop the area there are few obvious signs of it. However, the shop on the corner of Adams Row must have been unoccupied for some time as it has accumulated advertisements for events over a number of months - perhaps you paid your 6d (two and half pence) admission fee out of your pocket money to pick up some Christmas bargains and see Santa Claus at the Walsall Liberal Association's Christmas Fayre at the Blind Institute on Hatherton Road on Saturday, 23rd November 1963, or perhaps you were too old for Santa Claus and went to see the Northside Jazzmen at the Turf Hotel, Brownhills, on Friday 6th March 1964. Hawkins's old shop, opposite, is empty too, with a notice in the window directing customers to their new walk-round store further down Digbeth - in fact, in the building which later became an amusement centre. Clearly, the concept of letting customers wander round and make their own selection from the goods on display is catching on fast - Milletts, further up on the left, is already proudly advertising itself as a walk-round store. But changes more radical than that lie ahead for the shops in this part of Walsall.

Right: This must be one of the most radically altered streets in Walsall: Old Square as it used to be, looking towards Leicester Street. The clock tower, clearly visible and saying twenty past eleven in this photograph, cannot be seen from this angle now, although viewed from the other side it still rises elegantly above what has become the Leicester Street entrance to Old Square precinct. The shoppers who are here busy about their business, frowning in concentration as they stride along clutching their faithful old shopping bags - no throw-away plastic carriers in those days - probably see no reason to change Old Square; it provides a useful short cut from one part of Walsall to another, with some useful shops along the way, and shop windows to look in if you're not in any hurry. You could pick up your 'lively local paper', or have your hair done at Pat Granger's. One woman has a bunch of flowers; two young ladies are looking in SO Whitelegge's windows - dreaming of engagement rings and wedding rings, perhaps? Although many of the women are in coats and hats, the lady in the centre, like the young pair, seems quite happy in a summer dress, and the windows facing us at the end are open, so the weather is probably warm.

At work

Below: This photograph is recorded as having been taken in 1945, so there can be little doubt that the hundreds of union jacks and yards and yards of bunting which must have turned this factory into a blaze of colour are there in celebration of VE Day, 8th May. What thoughts are going through the heads of the workers as they take a minute off to pose for the photographer? Relief that it is all over, no doubt; happiness at the prospect of the return of loved ones or perhaps regret that peace has come to late to spare a lost son or husband; and perhaps above all a tremendous sense of achievement, because the efforts of every person here, both inside the factory and outside where many will have helped out as air-raid wardens, Red Cross workers, WVS and auxiliary firefighters, have all contributed to Victory. All over the country women have had to learn new skills and carry out arduous, taxing and sometimes dangerous work to keep industry and the war effort thriving. Now at last they can look forward to the prospect of things getting back to normal, though there is still work to be done to get the country's economy back onto its feet, and it will be more than nine years before they can finally tear up their ration books.

This fascinating scene of women at work dates from the early 1930s. This was Stammer's clothing factory in New Street, Walsall - and we can see from the photograph that they were clearly an extremely busy firm with a large output of work. These nimble-fingered machinists are producing men's suiting, and their overlooker is Alfred Turley. Back in the 1930s women's managerial capabilities had not been recognised, and though women often went out to work to supplement the family income the work was very often in factories and shops - and the manager was always a man! The work environment would perhaps raise a few eyebrows today, especially from a health and safety aspect. A closer inspection below the work tables reveals a system of wheels and rails; they probably connected the sewing machines, and we would want to know if these were moving parts!

A few more years would pass before women were needed to supplement every workforce, to take the place of men who had joined the services to fight in the second world war. After the war many of them didn't want to give up their jobs and go back to their old lives - they had become used to the independence that a weekly wage gave them. Life as we know it today, with women as well as men entering careers, had begun.

In the early days of electricity towards the end of the 19th century, when producing light just by flicking a switch must have seemed like magic, electrical current - at various voltages, sometimes AC and sometimes DC - was generated by many small powerhouses. During the first world war the government encouraged the development of fewer, larger suppliers, and in 1926 the Central Electricity Board was set up to build a national grid and supply electricity at a standardised voltage. A network of cables was laid to link the few huge power stations and carry electricity to all but the most remote places. These likely lads standing in the hole in Reedswood Park are working on the last joint in the cable which will complete the Great Electricity Scheme between Wolverhampton and Walsall. By the second world war most homes had electricity - but do you remember the plethora of different sockets and plugs that we had? A small item could run off a little 5-amp plug, while power-hungry apparatus like irons and kettles needed big fifteen-amp ones; and then of course you would want to plug a 5-amp plug into a fifteen-amp socket, so you would need an adaptor; then when the square-pinned 13-amp plugs arrived on the scene you needed even more adaptors so you could fit square plugs into round sockets as well as little plugs into big sockets. Eventually of course the 13-amp plug took over, and when people next had their houses rewired they could throw all their adaptors away and heave a sigh of relief.

Delivering the promise

Freshway UK and Freshway Farms is a well established family business run by the Burton family from Lower Farm in Stonnall. The Burtons took on their first farm in the area in 1812, the year that Napoleon made his disastrous foray into Russia. It is hard to imagine how empty the heath lands of the West Midlands were less than two centuries ago. A perusal of Ordnance Survey maps to study farm names will give easily-dated clues such as Quebec, Belle Isle and Trafalgar Farms throughout the region.

Apart from the difficult years known as the 'Hungry Forties' much of the nineteenth century was one of certainty, comfort and prosperity for Midland farmers. Son followed father whether as tenants on an estate or as yeomen working their own land.

Industrialisation and urbanisation brought about an increasing demand for local farm produce upon which the inhabitants of a district depended totally. The development of the railway system from the 1840s on made it possible for the first time for farmers to send dairy and arable produce to markets beyond the reach of horse-drawn wagons. Livestock were traditionally walked both to local and far distant markets, a practice which continued well into the inter-war years of the twentieth century.

Prior to 1914 farmers had been little affected by wars other than seeing better prices for their produce. Cecil Arthur Burton, like many countrymen experienced in handling horses, left home and fought in the Great War. He returned to the area in 1919, having won the Military Medal, second only to the Victoria Cross, for 'bravery in the field of battle when he had stayed, wounded, at his post while under heavy enemy fire'.

Two years later he was photographed proudly driving one of the early tractors with studded metal wheels. The plough being drawn was a converted horse plough with the handles still attached as specialist tractor ploughs had yet to be invented. Following these hopeful immediate post-war years, farming, beset by foreign imports and the Great Depression, degenerated into a 'dog and stick' state. Although land and buildings were neglected farmers survived, just, because they were much more self-sufficient and less cash-dependent than today. Family legend recalls the time when C A Burton Senior was

Top: C A Burton pictured on board an early tractor in 1921.
Right: The back-breaking task of harvesting cabbages in 1961.

fined for 'being drunk in charge of horse and cart' on his way home after market. In those more leisurely days many drivers of horse-drawn vehicles relied on the good sense of their horses and ponies to take them home through country lanes following after-work socialising.

The second world war brought jobs, hope and prosperity to many, including farmers, who had been hit by the Depression. Pasture and long-fallow land were put under the plough to increase production of the cereals, vegetables and animal feedstuffs that Britain could no longer import from the Empire and other countries.

In the 1940s C A Burton's son Cecil Arthur Burton Junior joined the family business on the edge of Walsall. He became the company's driving force for the next forty years, a period of greater change than ever before in one lifetime. Farming passed through the wartime phase of unheard-of government controls to become, in effect, part of

the post-war Welfare State. Post-war governments who had learned the lessons of the Depression were determined to provide the British housewife with affordable and plentiful food. They had also learned that industrial states depend upon farmers for their very existence and that Britain

Above and below: Two magnificent displays, at the Royal Show in the 1950s, of produce from the Staffordshire branch of the National Farmers Union of which C A Burton Senior was an active member.

the firm in 1979 the Burton family had become the largest independent cauliflower wholesaler in Britain. By the mid 80s the family farms had grown to 1800 acres (720 hectares), which made them the largest grower of gooseberries in Britain, producing nine percent of the national tonnage.

Locally Freshway Farms grow arable crops and vegetable crops such as sprouts, calabrese which is better known as broccoli, several varieties of cabbage and cauliflower. Today these vegetables are marketed through their own marketing system and also through major supermarket chains.

could not risk returning to the 'dog and stick' standards of low production of the 1930s any more than depend solely on foreign food.

During the years of growth and increasing individual prosperity following the war farmers catered for a growing population whose tastes were altered by travel and fashions. Today both supermarkets and television cookery programmes influence people's food purchasing habits in a manner undreamt of by early advertisers. The Burton family have kept abreast of these changes by ways which only farming families who consider stepping beyond the realms of food production can aspire to.

It was during the 'Swinging Sixties' that C A Burton Junior's two eldest boys, Jonathan and Gregory, bringing new ideas, joined their father and grandfather in running the family business.

On the crop production side the family had expanded their acreage not only in the West Midlands but also, in 1963, by buying the first of eight farms in the Land's End Peninsular of Cornwall.

The West Midland towns were once fed by the surrounding farmland but this is no longer the case. By purchasing land in Cornwall which enjoys a milder winter climate than the frost pockets of the Midlands the Burtons not only expanded their growing and marketing season but were able to command higher prices for fresh, out of season British produce, particularly new potatoes and cauliflowers. During the 70s the family expanded their Birmingham wholesaling operations first to market produce from more than 30 other Cornish farmers and latterly to import and market crops from Europe. By the time Robert, C A Burton Junior's third son, joined

Always alive to the need to diversify, the Burtons acquired the first of two retail fresh produce outlets in 1990 which now serves 9,000 people a week. Five years later they followed this with a new fresh foods enterprise that delivered high quality produce to various catering outlets across the Midlands from their own farms and from suppliers around the world. The new venture took off, and the large number of schools, factory canteens, fine hotels and restaurants who today serve Freshway UK's produce underlines its high quality.

By 1998 after acquiring several local businesses the company made an adventurous move to a spacious purpose-built facility. With room at their new premises to cater for today's needs as well as those of the future in a constantly expanding market, the Burtons look eagerly forward to continuing to 'deliver the promise' throughout the years to come.

Top: A state-of-the-art mobile vegetable packer pictured in 1998. *Below:* A modern temperature controlled delivery vehicle.

Owned and controlled by its members
The West Midlands Co-operative Society Ltd

How many of us remember that characteristic feature of shopping in years gone by - our 'divi number'? Millions of customers all over the country shared in the success of the Co-op, and passed on to their children a habit they had learned from their own parents. The Co-operative Society as a whole has a history that stretches right back to the early part of the 19th century. Today it still proudly proclaims the principles that inspired its beginnings - concern for the community, democracy, a mutual endeavour open to all - and continues to ensure for its many members a host of benefits, and a unique place in the hearts of ordinary British people.

The West Midlands Co-operative Society, as it is known today, dates back to the last century. There is evidence that as early as 1829 working people in Walsall were attracted to co-operative ideals as a means of improving their lot, and to establish a community where equality and mutuality held sway, for the good of all. But it was after the bold experiment of the Rochdale Pioneers that Co-operative retailing burst into life all over the North and Midlands of England. The Rochdale shop opened for business in December 1844. Its innovative founders bought goods in bulk - and therefore cheaply - which they sold to the public at large, who automatically became members of the Co-operative Society, sharing both in what profits accrued (through dividends) and in all decisions affecting the Society's operation. At first the shop offered only

four essential commodities - flour, butter, sugar and oatmeal - but in time the range of goods on offer was extended.

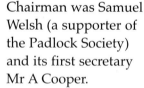

Walsall followed the pattern of many other towns in wanting to repeat the experiment for themselves. But the idea of working people running their own business in this way was revolutionary and an initial lack of confidence often beset their first efforts. The story of early Co-operative Societies is studded with examples of co-operation that barely get off the ground, but a passionate belief in the co-operative idea, and a conviction that Rochdale was not unique, sustained the determined few. In 1862, the 'Co-operator' newspaper refers to a Walsall Co-operative Society of 166 members, and in 1874 a Walsall Provident Co-operative Industrial Society came into being for a short spell, but it was the success of the Walsall Co-operative Padlock Society (a producer co-operative) that seems to have provided the real impetus for the establishment of the Walsall & District New Co-operative Society. A meeting in the YMCA lecture room on 10th August 1885 passed a resolution that a local co-operative retailing concern should be established - and Walsall has never looked back. Its first Chairman was Samuel Welsh (a supporter of the Padlock Society) and its first secretary Mr A Cooper.

Initial membership was rather small, around

Top right: William Millerchip, one of the principal figures associated with the Walsall Society and its President from 1896 to 1910. *Left:* Number 2 branch at Bloxwich, with the manager Mr Harrington pictured centre.

Right: An early picture of Branch number 7 at Walsall Wood.
Below: A line-up of the Milk Department staff, their horses and carts in front of the original Bridge Street premises.

thirty, and trading started in provisions in 1886 from a house in Hatherton Street then occupied by George Button, a riding saddle manufacturer who became a member of the Society's committee. Six months later, a lease was taken on a small shop at 226 Stafford Street and some progress followed, though it remained infuriatingly slow for some years. In 1887 the membership had grown to 45 and the share capital stood at £58, while annual sales totalled £547. By 1893, membership had reached 307, share capital £445 and annual sales amounted to £4,440. The generosity of the first Treasurer, George Harrison, did much to support the Walsall Co-op in its infancy, especially during teething problems with its first managers - one of whom even set up a shop in direct competition, after leaving his job! - and difficulties with supplies, some of which proved to be of inferior quality.

In the early 1890s, the Society moved to new premises at 243 Stafford Street and briefly ran a branch in Cadmore, before opening its first permanent branch in Palfrey in 1893. In 1895 educational work began (a strong feature of the Co-operative movement at the time) and in the same year the committee decided that the poor supply of bread had become intolerable and resolved that in future the Society should bake its own. A small bakery was acquired for £10 but more problems followed when a succession of bakers came and went - it was not until 1897 and the appointment of

a Mr Gwillam that bread began to pay its way in the business.

As the century drew to a close, there was much to celebrate. The Society had an established membership at last, was on a secure financial footing and the committee could turn their attention to expansion and diversification. At the AGM held in April 1899 the Society formally established its Education Committee. This new body set about organising activities - in Walsall there was to be a particular enthusiasm for musical and dramatic events - circulating Co-operative literature and running classes in Co-operation. In the years that followed the new committee was also to prove instrumental in establishing a widening network of Men's and Women's Guilds in the West Midlands. In the same year the Society, now thirteen years old, dropped the word 'new' from its name and set about a period of expansion which saw the opening of a new branch nearly every year. The product range, already extensive, now included boots and shoes, drapery, clothing and hardware. Coal was first on sale at this time, priced at 15 shillings (75p) per ton. In 1899 the Bloxwich branch began trading, in 1900 Pleck and Birchills were added to the list, followed by Paddock in 1902, Highgate and Walsall Wood in 1903

Left: The Society's float pictured at Walsall Carnival between the wars. *Below:* Digging out the bread delivery van following a heavy snowfall.

and Leamore, Croft Street and Butts in 1904. Also in 1904, a purpose-built store was completed in Bloxwich. Containing three separate shop units and a Co-operative Hall on the first floor its opening ceremony was a grand affair, attracting many dignitaries who were later entertained with tea and a concert. By 1906, when the Co-operative Congress came to Birmingham, the Walsall Society was attracting much praise. The Congress booklet speaks of it as 'in a sound financial condition, with every prospect of becoming one of the largest in Staffordshire'. As if to prove the point, in the following year the Society opened new purpose-built Central Premises in Bridge Street, attended by huge crowds including many of the Society's pioneers. In all respects it marked the coming of age of the Walsall & District Co-operative Society.

In 1914, at the outbreak of the first world war, the Society could proudly boast a membership of 9,367 and annual sales to the value of £130,903. The pace of development had become so dramatic that now not even the mighty buttress of war could halt its progress. Naturally there were problems, but plans already drawn up were pursued: in 1915 a dairy was built and brought into operation at the rear of Central Premises, the bakery and stables were improved and a programme of branch expansion enthusiastically adopted (Pleck Road and Stafford Street both opened branches in 1917). The Society's determination to secure supplies of agricultural produce saw the purchase of Ashcroft Farm and, in 1918, that of Lawton Grange Farm, both to be worked by the Society.

Above: Funeral procession viewed from Bridge Street, Walsall Co-op Masonary premises during the 1950s.

The aftermath of war proved more damaging. During three years of continuing shortages, prices rose - only to collapse in 1921 at the start of years of recession and unemployment. Profit margins were squeezed as never before, whilst dividends and interest on share capital had to be sustained in order to assure confidence. An employer with a social conscience as no other suddenly found itself unable to afford union rates of pay to its large workforce - and the spectre of redundancies loomed. But the Society was able to demonstrate remarkable resilience and - with wage cuts agreed - battled on. Indeed, 1921 saw the opening of grand premises in Sutton Coldfield and in the same year bottled milk was first on sale. The straitening economic climate also saw the Society introduce hire purchase as a method of payment - an innovation widely applauded by an impoverished membership.

By 1925, matters were improving and Walsall amalgamated with the Wednesbury Society, thereby adding several extra branches to its list. In 1928, four new branches opened their doors for the first time on the very same day! A buoyant mood was restored and enhanced by the amalgamation with the Cannock & District Society, formalised on 17 December 1928 and adding a further twelve branches to the total, along with 10,000 new members.

The 1930s saw the Society developing land on Shaw Street for its bakery and transport departments, and the construction of a warehouse and brand new dairy on Midland Road. Still more branches came into operation and in 1936 - the Society's Jubilee year - the funeral service was inaugurated, an important development which today has become a valued and reassuring presence in the form of 21 funeral homes throughout the region. The Society's Jubilee was celebrated in fine style with many of the 53,000 members taking an active part. Concerts, parties, excursions, even vehicle parades excited much interest - and there was a specially mounted exhibition in Walsall Town Hall, a published history of the Society, even the crowning of a Co-operative beauty queen!

The outbreak of war in 1939 marked a time of adjustment for the Society. As more and more male employees joined up or were conscripted, their places were taken by women. Co-operative Halls were requisitioned for the military, and the blackout, rationing and different opening hours all had to be contended with. But characteristically, the Society's turnover increased during this period - and still more branches opened (at Crankhall Lane, Pheasey, Druid's Heath and Bentley). In 1944, the centenary of the Rochdale Pioneers, the Walsall Society mounted a number of celebratory events, including the production of an ambitious theatrical production: 'The Pageant of the People' which played to packed houses at the Town Hall for three nights, and proved to be an unforgettable experience for all involved.

After the war, which claimed the lives of 20 employees and many more members, further branches were established and the coaching business taken up through the acquisition of Central Coachways in 1945. (The coach hire operation survived for forty years before being sold in the 1980s to

West Midlands Passenger Transport Executive.) Mobile shops - a butcher's and a grocery - first ran in 1949, whilst self-service was introduced in two branches initially, and extended throughout the network during the 1950s. In 1954, with a turnover of £5million and 78 shops, the Society welcomed its 100,000th member (a lady from Streetly). In November 1957 there was a grand reopening of the refurbished Central Premises - exactly 50 years (to the minute!) - after the building's first opening. The Vice-President, Arthur Evison, was proud to have attended both ceremonies, having started work for the Society all those years ago in September 1906.

By 1961, the year of its 75th birthday, the Society had become the 14th largest Co-operative Society in Britain, with a membership of 123,768, and annual sales topping £38 million in its 90 shops. And still it expanded. In 1966, Miss World officially opened a new three storey block of shops and offices in Lichfield Street. In 1970, which saw the introduction of dividend stamps, the Society took over its Rugeley counterpart, in 1972 absorbed the Wolverhampton Co-operative Society, and when, after lengthy debate, a merger was agreed with the Kidderminster Society in 1980, a new name was finally adopted: the West Midlands Co-operative Society.

The modern era has witnessed still more dynamic development. The Society's centenary celebrations in 1986 were swiftly followed by the

Above: The brochure produced to promote the Society's 75th Anniversary in 1961.
Left: President Tom Gwinnett and Secretary George Taylor congratulate Mrs Marjorie Ashton Garner on becoming the 100,000th member of the society.

- 21 funeral services, 16 pharmacies, 13 food stores, and 5 superstores across the region.

Innovation remains a vital feature of the West Midlands Co-operative Society, but it is still people who come first. The current Board of Directors are resolute in pursuing the Co-operative ideal. The President, H Withnall, and the Vice-President, Mrs D Shaw, in common with their fellow Directors - Miss F M Bate, B E Downing, Mrs I Edgar, N E Heywood, G E Hough, Ms H King, H S Minten,

opening of its biggest store to date - the superstore at Hawks Green, near Cannock. The presiding dignitary on this occasion proved most popular: Johnny Briggs (alias Mike Baldwin of Coronation Street). But while a move into supermarkets and a streamlining of image have done much to bring the Society up to date, holiday travel has provided a vision of the future. In 1996, the Society opened its first holiday store in Walsall. An idea developed with United Norwest Co-operative Society has since spawned many Co-op 'holiday hypermarkets' - a revolutionary approach to selling holidays. Each store offers a 'theatre of excitement' - replicas of major tourist destinations with interactive facilities including ski simulators and even an American Pontiac car - designed to make holiday purchase almost as thrilling as the holiday itself. So successful has the venture proved that in 1998 a business link-up with First Choice (the tour operator) was announced and a £20 million plan put into operation which will lead to 20 new such hyper-markets opening before the Millennium. Nowadays, the Society boasts - in addition to its holiday stores

B Naylor and G Taylor - all make strenuous efforts to ensure that the interests of the Society's 130,000 strong membership remain paramount, and positively encourage active participation from everyone in all aspects of the Society's operation and decision making (including the election of Directors). Co-operation is a beacon of good sense in a world often sullied by the appetites of ruthless big business. And only at the Co-op do profits genuinely benefit everyone - management, workforce and customers - because every individual has a stake in this remarkable, and enduring, triumph.

Above: The Members Reunion dinner in 1957. **Below left:** *Fiona Florists, Gillity Road, Walsall as it is today.* **Below:** *A modern fleet of Co-op funeral limousines.*

From horseshoes to North Sea gas rigs

William Sharp set up in Aston in 1850 with a general smithy and farrier's shop. Like many such small businesses it changed its products to suit changing markets. Unlike the majority of backyard workshops in the nearby Black Country, Sharp's had the space to produce ornamental wrought iron gates. These were made both to order and on spec to cater for the burgeoning mercantile classes of late Victorian England who wished to emulate the landed classes by showing off splendid gates and railings around their homes.

The company passed to William Sharp the Second and then to his son in law, a Mr Brindley, during which time the works were moved to James Watt Street in Birmingham. Little is known of company history in the early twentieth century but by the 1930s the company was established in premises in Thimble Mill Lane with a staff of half a dozen.

Decline had set in to such an extent that William Bartley Sharp, the commission salesman was owed £250, the equivalent then of a year's pay for senior clerks. To settle this debt Mr Brindley gave the company, lock stock and barrel to his employee who continued trading in iron gutter brackets and the like for builders.

Following a year's illness W B Sharp died in 1940, leaving the company to his widow. She was unable to keep it going due to the difficulties of obtaining supplies for un-essential non-war work. All the men had either been called up into the armed forces or directed into essential war work. By the end of 1941 William Sharp was struggling and up for sale.

It was at this unhappy stage in its history that Sharps was saved by the entry of Jack Horton, a

"To settle the debt Mr Brindley gave the company, lock stock and barrel to his employee"

Below: *William Sharp Ltd's second premises pictured shortly after opening in 1943.*

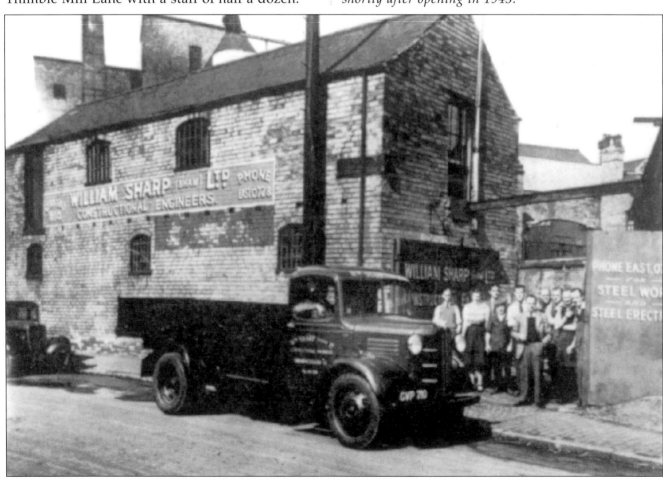

until their first new customer ordered a few pipe brackets. This was the seed from which the present company grew to prominence. Other heating engineers in Birmingham were attracted to William Sharp during the war while 'under new management'. As Jack Horton enjoyed his lecturing income his new venture was at an advantage in not having to pay his salary. It even had a surplus in the bank. Unfortunately it had been sold with such a non-existent credit rating that one of the suppliers recommended changing its name; this was a challenge to the new owner who rejected the advice.

Chartered Engineer working in Structural Design and doing part time lecturing at the local technical colleges. In those days such work left ample time to run a business on a part time basis. By chance he bought a copy of the Evening Mail in which he saw an advertisement for 'A Builders' Ironworks Manufacturers' for sale. Obtaining access from the vendor's solicitors he visited the near-derelict workshops, staffed by a £5/week septuagenarian blacksmith. The equipment too was overdue for pensioning off while stock consisted of 3cwt of steel bars worth under £3.

To his surprise the vendor's solicitor treated his offer of £150 for the company with derision. Mr Horton persisted through his own solicitor, who eventually got the offer accepted some months after Jack Horton had forgotten the whole business! When the new owner took over on a Saturday - then a working day - in 1941, all portable items had disappeared. His partner Arthur Ranson started the line shaft from which all the machinery was powered and the excited but inexperienced purchaser nearly lost a finger when testing the power drill.

On the next Monday he and Frank, the ancient blacksmith, idly chatted

Top left: Drawing office staff in 1978. **Right:** *William Sharp Ltd's Cricket Club pictured in 1978.*

By 1943 William Sharp was employing two men, one of whom was Ernie, a part time farm worker famous for arriving late but making up for it by working like a Trojan well into the evenings. It was at this stage that the company won a war work contract to produce lifting straps and packaging fitments for engine packing cases. The first half of the order was made at a loss so all the old machines were sold for scrap and the factory re-equipped. Following this the price of seventy shillings (£3.50) per set of fitments enabled the company to profit from this contract for the next few years. Labour being scarce, fourteen casual workers staffed the night shift to get the job done.

During these developing years Les Smith, a plater out of work due to illness, took over as Works Manager and reorganised the whole system. The war years brought out the best in Britain when we had to improvise and make do with whatever we could get. Quite different from the current passion for political correctness and all that means!

By the war's end William Sharp had a greatly improved reputation and a work force of ten. Like many companies that had changed direction during the war Sharp's found that peace brought its own problems of what to do in the future.

The decision was made to leave the manufacture of plumbing requisites and enter the Structural Steel Trade. This was based on the pre-war experience of most of the staff. The skilled manpower existed to make the change but the Thimble Mill Lane factory was totally unsuitable, being too small, too low and lacking cranes. Nothing daunted, the workforce set to work producing prefabricated steel structures as large as the limitations of the site and their combined muscle power permitted. This was still an age when industrial workers could take pride in their physical prowess at work.

It was a triumph for a firm which only a few short years before had been held in poor repute, that the hard stretched Ministry of Supply granted a licence to Sharp's to build a new factory in the days when all materials were

Top: Ron Kelsey presents Stan Smith's retirement present in 1984.
Right: A long span walkway at RAF Uphaven.

rationed! The company bought four acres of land at Bescot Crescent from Walsall Corporation. Construction started in 1947, the year of that desperately hard winter when housewives queued to fill their prams with coal. The new works enjoyed the advantages of height and space served by overhead gantries and cranes. These enabled the production of large steel beams for the post-war Contemporary style of architecture in which vitally needed blocks of flats, many schools and shopping centres were quickly built of concrete-clad steel-framed buildings taller than anything ever seen in Britain.

From this new departure William Sharp has expanded to become well-known specialists in the manufacture and erection on site of structural steel frames not only for buildings of all types but also of much of the equipment infrastructure within. Local authority clients require buildings as diverse as hospitals, swimming pools, schools and civic centres. Each of these has specialist needs for heating, movement of people, wastes and equipment etc. Other specialist clients catered for are the demanding moguls of the oil and chemical, coal and steel industries whose

structures are subject to the attrition not only of the elements of land, sea and air but to the corrosive nature of some of their products.

The founders of the firm of farriers and general smiths from which this all began would be astounded at the diversity and sheer enormity of the fabrications made from the same raw material which they once hammered out by hand using the simplest of tools.

From the 1960s Sharps went into the Stockholding business as distributors throughout Britain from the Midlands and South Wales to the Thames for Robertsons "Q" Gratings. This valuable flooring material is now manufactured at Bescot Crescent.

Equipment made to order varies from salt hoppers for the Department of Transport to access walkways, "Q" gratings, for North Sea gas rigs. Unusual orders include one for the civil engineers Laing which required two twenty-six ton movable floors for a Jacobean style country house in the Home Counties; not surprisingly these were delivered in pieces for installation on site. More local contracts 'open to the public' are the indoor Market Forum at Cannock and motorway road bridges near Burton on Trent.

The company motto could well be 'anything, anywhere'. Wherever the reader travels they will see steel structures, both clad and bare, made by William Sharp for a variety of jobs in every industry, including the steel industry which provides the raw materials from which everything is made. The craftsman bricklayer has truly been outpaced by the mass production techniques of the large scale prefabricated building industry.

The company was led through the post-war period by a team comprising Jack Horton as Managing Director and Ron Kelsey, a former pre-war trainee draughtsman now running the Contracts department. The Smith brothers commanded in the workshops with Les as Works Director and Stan as Foreman. The template shop was in the capable hands of Albert Brassington

Top right: An aerial view of the premises with the M6 at the top left of the picture. *Below left:* Morrisons superstore at Walsall. *Below:* The erection of the main girders at Tipton Leisure Centre in 1998.

Engineering, joined his father's team. He instituted the installation of new machines such as the Kaltenbach saw, Cocksedge drilling line and Vernet automated angle punch and cropper with which to increase productivity of standardised components trimmed, when necessary, to order.

The expanding company built a second storey of offices which provided welcome space for a larger drawing office. In the late 1960s Philip Horton, following three years at Braithwaites, entered the works under the aegis of Les Smith. His brother David, a Chartered Accountant, joined the family weighted management team in 1974. Sharp's has been strengthened by this gradual assimilation of the second-generation directors taking over from the post-war Founder Fathers as each in turn retired. A far cry from the rather desperate days when Les Smith became Works Manager for Jack Horton who had gambled on buying a derelict company.

*Above: Construction in progress for Metrabrasive, Bilston. **Below:** Tipton Sports Academy.*

while a newcomer George Davis took charge of on-site erections. This team ran Sharps for some twenty years of unparalleled expansion with world famous clients and others throughout a Britain enjoying low inflation and a thriving economy.

New buildings counted by the acre were manufactured and erected to the order of Dunlop Rubber, Kodak the photographic people and Lucas of car electrics fame. Other prestigious clients included Amalgamated Electrical Industries now part of the vast General Electricity Company, Forgings and Press Work in heavy industry and the wide spread Midland Red Omnibus Company empire. Such free-spending clients required modern well-lit airy buildings with minimal obstruction from unnecessary roof supports.

Such expansion was reflected by Sharp's own need for increased space in the mid 1960s when three huge new bays added 45,000 square feet, approximately 5,000 square metres, of extra manufacturing space. In 1964 John Robert Horton, a graduate in Structural

The year 1970 saw dramatic changes in the industrial building market, partly due to the oil crisis which fuelled the inflation which led to a decline, even collapse, of old-established industrial clients. Those who had ordered and re-ordered from Sharp's in previous decades tightened their belts and stopped expanding. William Sharp Ltd had to look for other clients in the new industrial areas such as the M4 Corridor or Silicon Valley, as the Thames Valley was nick-named, and the South East. Warehouses of lighter construction were the order of the day to reduce costs and attract clients such as Brixton and Slough Estates Companies.

The trend of dying heavy industry and developing new light industries, and of established organisations changing from traditional brick buildings to prefabricated industrial-style accommodation, provided an expanding market for an experienced firm like Sharp's.

The present client base includes hospitals and prisons, superstores and football grounds, where adaptability on the part of the supply and erection contractor is vital.

The people who work for Sharp's can look around their own region with pride. Tipton Sports Academy and Walsall Football Club are as regularly visited as Morrison's Superstore while the Anchor Brook Business Park is a standing advertisement to all who go about their daily work in a Sharp-designed and constructed environment.

Come the Millennium, William Sharp (Structural) Ltd will celebrate their 150th year of trading in memorable style, ready to step into the Twenty-First Century with confidence in their ability to maintain a solid foundation of 'any thing, any where'.

Below: Coombs Bridge at Halesowen.

"WILLIAM SHARP (STRUCTURAL) LTD WILL CELEBRATE THEIR 150TH YEAR OF TRADING IN MEMORABLE STYLE"

'Deeds not words' - a recipe for success

'Hard work brings success' had long been school teacher and designer Dorothy Bryan's maxim, which she effectively put into practice when she purchased Hydesville back in 1952.

The semi derelict building on Broadway North had caught her eye the previous year, and its potential for development into a school quickly fired her creative imagination. Backed by a group of good friends who invested in the venture, she made arrangements to acquire the substantial building - built by former Mayor and noted Spiritualist Mr Venables - then quite literally rolled up her sleeves and got busy. She painted walls, ceilings, windows and doors, swept and washed the floors and did 1001 necessary jobs, rubbing and polishing until the whole building shone like a new pin. Desks and blackboards were moved in; 'chalk and talk' were the accepted teaching methods back in the early 1950s, so apart from books little else was needed in the way of equipment - a far cry from the multi-media technology the school enjoys today!

Dorothy Bryan had previously qualified as a teacher of Art and Elocution and worked as a peripatetic teacher for Walsall LEA, also teaching Elocution to a number of private pupils around the town. A talented artist and designer, Miss Bryan designed carpets for some of the factories in Kidderminster, including Brintons.

By 1952 Hydesville Tower School was ready to take its first pupils. Working alongside Miss Bryan in the new venture was

Left: Dorothy Flood, neé Bryan, who founded the school in September 1952. Right: Miss E M Flint, Co-Principal who later was to become Mayor of Walsall. Below: The school viewed from its gardens in the late 1950s.

Express & Star, Wolverhampton

Miss E M Flint, who had taught Art at Queen Mary's School in Walsall.

The school that was destined for high achievement through to senior level started as a kindergarten and preparatory school with a total of 21 children. Miss Bryan worked within the school as bursar or business manager while Miss Flint was responsible for the curriculum; in addition the two founders taught their own specialist subjects. In 1953 Mr A C Scott became the Senior Master, remaining in the position for eleven years. Mr William Flood took over as headmaster in 1967, and was succeeded in 1983 by Mr and Mrs David Farrell, the present principals.

The school grew and developed over the years, and with its expansion adjoining buildings were acquired as they became available. Number 23 Broadway North was purchased in 1973 and number 29 in 1987, though the original building, number 25, remains effectively the centre of the school. A gradual change in direction towards

"PUPILS FROM OVERSEAS HAVE OVER THE YEARS ADDED THEIR OWN SPECIAL INPUT INTO THE LIFE OF THE SCHOOL"

accepting a wider age range of children also came about, and the appropriate teaching resources were added as the school moved on.

In the late 1950s the key decision was taken to open a secondary department which in 1965 was widened to develop the sciences. More elaborate equipment was acquired together with the necessary specialist subject staff. Computers were installed in the 1980s to provide pupils with what was increasingly becoming a vital grounding in new technology.

The school's lower age group was extended in 1984, when a specialist nursery unit was built and furnished with play equipment, and three-year-olds were for the first time welcomed into the school.

Pupils from overseas have over the years added their own special input into the life of the school.

Above: Some of the younger children hard at work during the late 1950s.

Above: Part of the New Technology building.

Occasionally students from Hong Kong have been welcomed to Hydesville, and during the 1980s Iranian students - most of them charming young men - joined the school, an arrangement which ended with the fall of the Shah's regime.

However, local parents seeking a good education for their children also recognise the opportunities presented by Hydesville. At 11+ and at senior levels, the school offers an excellent preparation for selective academic education. There is an outstanding record of places obtained at 11+ and 6th Form at local Grammar Schools and also at King Edward's School, Edgbaston. From the latter school especially, many former Hydesville pupils have progressed to Oxford and Cambridge Universities.

Walsall and the surrounding areas are served by the school, and coaches bring children from Bloxwich, Hammerwich, Four Oaks, Little Aston, Sutton Coldfield, Handsworth Wood, West Bromwich and Darlaston.

Drama and music particularly flourish with cups being won by the school choirs at Catshill, Dudley and Cheltenham Festivals. Over the last fifteen years the school has been awarded no less than

eight trophies at the ISA Drama Festivals, as well as four best actor awards. A particular achievement was being chosen to be one of the supporting choirs in the Phillip Schofield production of 'Joseph and the Amazing Technicolor Dreamcoat' at Birmingham Hippodrome in early 1994. One of the school's earliest drama successes in the days when Miss Bryan and Miss Frith taught Elocution was stage and television star Andrew O'Connor. Andrew revisited the school in late 1994 when he was starring in 'Me and My Girl' at the Hippodrome in Birmingham. Fine achievements in athletics, swimming and team sports such as rugby, soccer, cricket and hockey have also been recorded.

Back in the 1950s Dorothy Bryan introduced Elocution and Art - her own disciplines - to the syllabus, and the subjects still feature high on today's school curriculum. In the January 1998 LAMDA Speech examinations, eighty-six per cent of the entrants gained Distinction or Honours. The school has its successes too in Art and Textiles, and the Tomlinson Art Competition and the ISA Midlands Competition lists a number of prizewinners from Hydesville Tower.

This kind of prizewinning success is reinforced by the examination results achieved by the students. Over the period 1993-98 an average of seventy-five per cent of Year 11 pupils achieved five or more A to C passes, a statistic well above the national GCSE average, and one of which both staff and pupils can be proud. The 1998 Higher Grade pass rate in French was a splendid 100 per cent, and 100 per cent pass rates were also recorded in German, Music, Physical Education, Sociology and Religious Studies. More than 80 per cent of entries in

Chemistry, English Literature, History, Physics and Art also achieved Higher Grade passes.

The school's emphasis on the development of personal self-confidence is reflected by the staff's firm belief in valuing each pupil as an individual. Class size is kept deliberately small so that each child can be noticed and his or her personal abilities recognised and developed. Hydesville's structured and well-disciplined community adds an important dimension to the high academic standards that the children regularly achieve, cultivating self discipline built upon personal integrity and care and consideration for others.

A very active Parent Association organises numerous activities during the school year raising funds and providing equipment of all kinds, and most importantly a new mini bus in 1997 which is of benefit to every child in the school. The 1998 summer fete organised by the PTA raised more than £4,000 in spite of bad weather.

Hydesville has come a long way since the 'chalk and talk' days of the 1950s. Today science, technology and information technology feature highly on the school's timetable. Computing facilities are available to all the pupils, and a specialist information

technology unit offers the opportunity to keep abreast of today's developments. Even the junior classes have their own computer with multi-media access to encyclopaedias, and television and video facilities are available across the entire school. A video surveillance system lends security and confidence to the school premises. Future plans include more extensive library facilities and improved dining arrangements.

The basic principles on which Hydesville Tower School was founded still hold good today. When Dorothy Bryan designed a badge for the school more than 45 years ago she incorporated into it the elements of her own recipe for success: the hill for endeavour, the tower for strength, the lion for courage, the owl for wisdom and the rising sun for hope. The school's motto, 'Facta

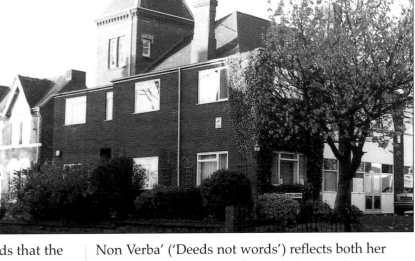

Non Verba' ('Deeds not words') reflects both her own achievements and those of Hydesville Tower School's pupils down the years. Indeed when the freak storm of January 1990 almost removed the roof from the school's landmark Tower the current principals insisted that it must be replaced with brickwork exactly matching the Edwardian originals.

Mr and Mrs Farrell and their staff can today be justifiably proud of the students who leave Hydesville Tower as confident, well-balanced young men and women - and the School's commitment is to go forward into the next millennium with continued dedication to the highest possible standards.

Top left: The refurbished tower roof being repositioned by crane. Above: The finished result.

At the top of the saddlemaking tree

Frank Baines Saddlery is a family firm that has connections with the equestrian trade going back 200 years.

Frank grew up listening to his grandfather's fascinating tales of days gone by, one of which described how his grandfather's grandfather, as a boy of thirteen, had walked from Laysters in Hertfordshire, with his mother, to Walsall where he was left to learn the trade. Other tales were of the old saddlemakers his grandfather had known, their methods and practices and the way they worked and lived.

The stories his grandfather told fired young Frank with the ambition to work in the same field himself, and in 1962 the young man started work as an apprentice with saddler Enoch Antill. After twelve years with the company he moved to a newly formed Walsall company, Falcon Saddlery, and became involved in the design and making of new saddles, at times working with top equestrian names such as the late Caroline Bradley, for whom he designed and produced a new saddle. Frank's ability to understand the individual needs of the horse and rider was to become an important part of his future success and reputation.

Saddlemaking is a complex art at which Frank was to become a master, and involves many processes, the first of which is to create the 'tree' or frame on which the saddle is built. Once the tree is complete, nylon webbing is stretched and fitted to it to give a firm, sprung base to the seat. Latex foam is today used instead of the traditional serge for the padding, and over this a piece of hide is fastened to the tree to create the seat. Skirts are then fitted which cover the metal fittings for the stirrup leathers, and the girth straps are attached before the saddle flap. The panel is the final part of the process, providing a wool-filled cushion between the tree and the horse's back. The woollen filling ensures that the thickness can be regulated to suit the shape of the horse's back.

During the process of making a saddle an incredible 15 metres of machining and around 850 hand stitches are made using many types of thread and needles. Around 400 pins and tacks are hammered into each saddle, and up to 90 pieces of leather, webbing, foam and metal are put together to make the finished article.

"Equipment is only as good as the craftsmanship which goes into its manufacture, the materials from which it's made, and the care it receives during use," says Frank. "The use of inferior materials can

Below: Frank working on a saddle in the Walsall Leather Museum.

produce economies - but they will result in less satisfactory products."

A prestigious competition was staged in 1979, sponsored by the Worshipful Company of Saddlemakers of the City of London. The set task was to make a leather jumping saddle, and the entire process, from choosing the materials to the completion of the saddle, would be taken into consideration by the judges.

Frank entered - and won - the competition. The award was a turning point in Frank's career, and as a result he went on to establish a reputation as one of the top craftsmen in his trade. Following his success, he began to consider setting up his own business and with his

wife Jane, a skilled leather machinist, formed Frank Baines Saddlery of Walsall on November 1st 1983. Business grew steadily through 1984 and 85 and Frank and Jane began exhibiting their saddlemaking skills at agricultural and horse shows both at home and abroad and also succeeded in winning the Saddlemaker of the Year competition for the third time in five years. Thus ended a successful year with order books full for 1986.

To cope with the growing demand, Frank had to find another saddlemaker to join the firm and

Top: *Frank and Keith Richardson attaching the girth straps to a saddle.* *Left:* *The Princess Royal presenting one of Frank's saddles to Ian Stark, winner of Badminton in 1987.*

Left: Frank's wife Jane sewing a saddle flap.
Below: Shaun Jacombs and Frank Baines choosing the leather for a saddle.

To complement the saddlemaking side of the business Frank decided to start a section manufacturing high quality bridlework which was set up in 1988 with top craftsman Michael Citrullo in charge. The company was becoming too large for the premises on Whittimere Street and by March 1988 they moved to Northcote Street. Frank began to expand his workforce, employing two saddlemakers he had worked with previously, Keith Richardson and Peter Lyons, both of whom went on to take awards in the Saddlemaker of the Year competition.

was lucky enough to persuade Jeremy Rudge to join them. Frank had worked with Jeremy prior to setting up his own company and he had a high opinion of his saddlemaking abilities. This confidence in Jeremy's craftsmanship was rewarded when he won the 1986 Saddlemaker of the Year award, whilst Frank was second.

1990 was another eventful year for the saddlery with Frank becoming a Freeman and later a Liveryman of the Worshipful Company of Saddlers. He also earned the Freedom of the City of London in the September of that year.

saddlemaking to ensure that a full understanding of the requirements of the many individual equestrian disciplines is met. Frank has worked closely with such riders as Stephen Clarke, Chris Bartle and Ian Stark from the Dressage and Three Day Event world, and he has designed polo saddles for Major Ronald Ferguson, to name but a few.

Frank Baines Saddlery currently export their saddles and bridles to many countries world-wide, including Sweden, Finland, Denmark, Norway, Holland, Italy, Switzerland, Germany, Spain, Cyprus, Japan, Chile, Jamaica, Australia, USA and Canada and as a result of this became a winner of the Birmingham Post's European Award for Export in 1991.

Walsall has long been recognised as a centre for traditional craftsmanship in leather goods and saddlemaking but to remain successful Frank Baines Saddlery work extremely hard to maintain high standards and meet delivery dates. Nothing is more likely to reduce standards than introducing production line methods. Therefore every product from Frank Baines is the responsibility of one individual saddler or bridlemaker from design to the finished item and many hours of time and skill are invested to ensure the high quality of the finished product. The company sells everything it produces but doesn't intend to cut corners to increase productivity and with Frank and Jane's children Garry and Victoria as part of the firm the family looks set to succeed in the saddlery trade well into the next century.

Top left: Frank being introduced to the Princess Royal in 1990. Below: Frank Baines' staff from left to right: Shaun Jacombs, Frank, Peter Lyons, Ian Hopkins, Keith Richardson, Victoria Baines, Simon Woolley and Jane Baines.

As orders began to grow following the move to larger premises the company needed to expand the workforce again, but there was a shortage of skilled leather-workers, so Frank decided to set up a training scheme for new staff to gain the necessary skills to take the National Skill Assessment and Qualification Scheme for Saddlers. Five new staff were recruited to the scheme in 1991, some of whom were trainees from Walsall Leatherworks College. Frank's ability to pass on his skills, coupled with the company's commitment to the development of individual craftsmanship, led to Frank Baines Saddlery being awarded the first National Training Award to be won by the saddlery industry - accomplished in competition with 1575 other companies. The award was presented to Frank by His Royal Highness the Prince of Wales. This is not the only royal connection; however, in 1990 one of Frank's saddles was presented to the Princess Royal on behalf of the Riding for the Disabled Association, and Frank met the Princess Royal again a few weeks later when she visited Walsall to open the Leathergoods Museum and Frank was called upon to demonstrate his saddlemaking skills during the visit.

Close liaison with top riders world-wide and a great depth of knowledge of the anatomy of horses is an essential part of

Cliff-Barnsby Saddlery - still riding high after 200 years

The dynasty founded by George Cliff more than 200 years ago almost foundered several times over in those days long ago when virtually every family, especially those living in poverty, had more than one child who died in infancy.

George, who worked in the leather trade, lived in Badger's Yard in Park Street, where he made leather breeches. He and his wife Elizabeth had five children, four boys and a girl. In 1793 his son, thirteen-year-old George followed his father into the trade and began his apprenticeship in bridle preparing. In time his own son Jabez, whose brothers and sisters all died in infancy, carried on the family tradition.

At that time horses were virtually the only form of transport, carrying both goods and people, and the saddler and bridlemaker occupied a position of prime importance. In 1873 the enterprising young Jabez Cliff started up his own saddlery business, Jabez Cliff & Co Ltd, in Portland Street, Walsall. Less than ten years later, however, tragedy struck. Jabez Cliff and his two sons Samuel and George all died during the typhoid epidemic that swept across Britain in 1881. Marshalling their determination - and their own abilities in the trade - his wife and daughter Mary kept the business going until Mary married skilled

bridlemaker Frederick Tibbits in 1882. Their only son Jabez Cliff Tibbits joined the company in 1902 - a move that was destined to be central to the company's success.

Above: Jabez Cliff, the founder of the company.
Top right: The original premises on Portland Street where Jabez Cliff & Co was started in 1873. Right: The Globe Works pictured in 1926.

Not far from the Cliff factory were the premises of the world renowned saddle making company J A Barnsby & Sons, who were situated at Globe Works in Lower Forster Street, and in 1906 the young Jabez Cliff Tibbits pulled off an amazing coup when he put in a daring bid for the firm. Their offer was accepted, and the two companies amalgamated. Jabez Cliff & Co Ltd saddles retained the prestigious Barnsby label, whilst the high quality bridles were manufactured under the Cliff name, thus creating the saddlery brand name 'Cliff-Barnsby'.

Their main export markets were Germany and Russia - an unfortunate position for a company to be in during the decade that saw the international tensions which eventually led to the outbreak of the Great War in 1914. With sound judgment Jabez Cliff Tibbits realised that the time had come to diversify into other areas of the leather trade. The company began to manufacture a wide range of sports products and leather goods, turning out cricket and other hard and soft balls, golf bags and holdalls,

travel goods and leather cases. In the early 1920s Jabez Cliff Tibbits was appointed managing director.

During the decade of the 1920s the company patented the 'Globe' non-tear football. The innovative new ball proved to be a further feather in the firm's cap, gaining fame when it was used in four FA Cup Finals and the 1928 Olympic Games.

The years of the second world war saw a change of direction for the company towards the production of bren gun pouches, ammunition belts, webbing and leather goods for the Ministry of Defence. The links with the military that began during the 1940s continued to flourish through the years. When British task forces in the Falklands realised that the country's inhospitable

Above: The Cliff non-tear football used in the 1931 Wembley Cup Final. Below: Her Majesty the Queen being presented with Cliff-Barnsby saddles for her eldest children during her visit to Walsall in 1961. Inset: The late Tom Tibbits with current Company President Oliver Morton examining the tack to be presented to Prince Charles and Princess Anne.

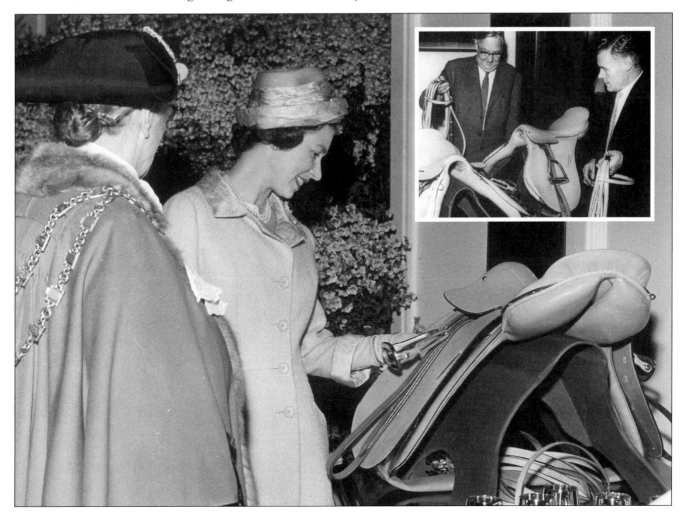

terrain called for four-legged transport, it was to Jabez Cliff & Co Ltd that they turned with their urgent request for pack saddlery so that vital equipment and weapons could be transported by mules. The company was later honoured by Her Majesty the Queen, who in 1990 awarded Jabez Cliff & Co the Royal Warrant as Saddler and Loriner.

The Company's capabilities include the manufacture of saddlery equipment to the prestigious military units of the Kings Troop, Royal Horse Artillery, the Household Cavalry, the Metropolitan Police and the City of London Police. They supply military units throughout the world with ceremonial equipment.

Jabez Cliff Tibbits was knighted in 1948 by King George VI for his services to the town, and from that day on was known in the town as 'Sir Cliff'. During his lifetime Sir Cliff became a well-known and respected man in the community, and was elected Mayor of Walsall in 1939. Re-elected for a second term in 1940, he achieved the rank of Alderman of Walsall the following year. Sir Cliff lived on until 1974

Though the company has seen many changes and developments over the years, younger descendants of George Cliff have continued to join the family firm, with the name Cliff becoming traditional within the family. Now into its seventh generation, Jabez Cliff & Company Ltd is well established as a traditional family firm in the true sense of the word.

Today, the company represents one of the biggest saddlery businesses in the UK, and is among the top five in the world. Barnsby has remained at the forefront in the saddlery trade for many years. They believe that their reputation for excellence lies in their experience over two centuries, the expertise of their staff, and in the high quality of the goods they produce.

Today the company's main markets abroad include the USA, Western Europe, the Far East, Africa, the Middle East, Australia and the Pacific Rim, and their export goods include sporting goods, luggage, high quality golf equipment, saddlery and other fine leather goods. The company's export achievements were officially recognised when they were awarded third place in the Walsall Chamber's exporter of the year competition. Their main customers, however, remain in the equestrian industry, and their quality products are used by many leading professional riders. Showjumpers John and Michael Whitaker, Nick Skelton and Di Lampard all ride with Cliff-Barnsby saddlery, as do eventers Mary King and Ginny Elliot (Leng) and dressage riders Anky Van Grunsven and Richard Davison.

Honesty in endeavour, a job well done, and the firm's commitment to manufacturing goods of unsurpassed quality have greatly contributed to Cliff Barnsby's success. A certificate from Walsall TEC underlines the company's forward thinking attitude to the use of modern manufacturing techniques, and the team is already planning to adopt further state of the art technology in the future to continue to increase their efficiency. At the same time they aim to uphold in the years to come the high standards that have seen the company through the last two centuries.

Top left: Sir Cliff Tibbits. Above: Captain Mark Phillips opening the factory extension in 1979 with former chairman Edwin Hickton. Below: HRH the Princess Royal on her visit to Globe Works in 1992 with Jennifer, Kent, Pixie and Cliff - all of whom are direct descendants of George Cliff.

Good health to the customer

Sandwell Library

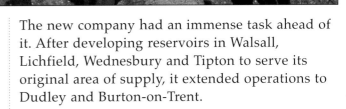

In 1853, the Black Country was densely populated and the coal, iron and steel industries were booming, but the lack of a reliable supply of healthy water was becoming critical. Quite apart from the personal misery caused, a workforce struck by cholera and typhus could not maintain full productivity. Previous attempts to improve water supplies had failed, principally because of a lack of financial backing, but in 1852 a civil engineer, John Robinson McClean, managed to gather together a small group of men who were prepared to subscribe to an undertaking to provide a proper water supply to the district.

The South Staffordshire Water Work Company was created by Act of Parliament in 1853, but in spite of the obvious need for a water supply it took time for sufficient money to be raised and the necessary works put in place. Following the enactment of the Bill, an office was established at Lichfield Railway Station in 1853, and the official opening of the South Staffordshire Waterworks took place five years later in Walsall.

The new company had an immense task ahead of it. After developing reservoirs in Walsall, Lichfield, Wednesbury and Tipton to serve its original area of supply, it extended operations to Dudley and Burton-on-Trent.

During the following years, the South Staffordshire Waterworks Company moved its offices to Paradise Street, Birmingham, and continued to open new depots and extend the catchment area for customers. A succession of

Top left: Brunswick Park in 1898, with Wood Green Pumping Station in the background. Top right: Workmen laying pipeline. Below left: Bridgeman Street Depot, Walsall, 1922. Below right: A Cornish Beam Engine at Wood Green.

Acts of Parliament allowed funds to be raised to build more pumping stations and reservoirs. Steam had been used to power the pumping stations, but electrification began after the establishment of the national grid.

Supplying water to Walsall
An open reservoir was first built at Moat Hill, Walsall with work commencing on the 12th November 1856, and it was eventually converted into covered reservoirs in 1936. They served Walsall and Bloxwich until 1994 when they were taken out of service.

Following the completion of works in 1858 it was necessary to provide distribution mains and service pipes. Rates and regulations records from the first water regulations booklet at the time show that the average cost of providing a service was ten shillings. Water rates to the Company were payable quarterly in advance and were based on the Annual Value of the premises. A property valued between £4 and £5 would face a quarterly charge of 1s.8d and a property valued at £100 would be charged £1.5s.0d. Additional charges were made for each private bath at 2s.0d per quarter and if more than one closet was installed an extra 1s.0d per quarter was charged.

Walsall's first store and reporting base during the 1860s was a stable at the rear of John McClean's house in Park Street. Much larger premises were required as the Company grew and a move was made in 1895 to a substantially built residence situated at the corner of Bridgeman Street and

Pleck Road, Walsall, known locally as Bridgeman House. The house was part occupied by John McClean's brother-in-law J Newsome who was Chief Accountant of the South Staffordshire Railway and another part of the house was used by John McClean to train students of engineering. South Staffordshire Water Works purchased the property as it was ideally suited to the Company's needs, and it continued to be known as the Walsall Depot until its closure in 1981 when the staff were moved to a new reporting base at the headquarters in Green Lane.

The Company had decided during the 1930s that underground supplies had been developed to the maximum and so a major reservoir had been planned near Rugeley. Construction was delayed until after World War II and Blithfield Reservoir was opened by the Queen Mother in 1953. The electrification programme was also resumed, with a string of booster stations being built to supply water to the higher parts of the area.

More recent schemes have included the River Severn Scheme, which became necessary because the demands of the domestic

Top left: Raising the 22" cast iron main at Highbridge, Pelsall in August 1927. *Centre:* A Garrett Steam Lorry, one of several that worked hard delivering slack to the pumping stations that required up to 3 tons of coal a day to keep the engines pumping water. *Below:* The underground reservoir at Barr Beacon, constructed in 1899 and still in use today.

consumer and industry continued to rise. The project involved the creation of Clywedog Reservoir in the Severn basin in Wales and Chelmarsh Reservoir and Hampton Loade Treatment Works near Bridgnorth, Shropshire, and the engineering aspects of this scheme aroused much interest in the early 1960s, when they were seen as practically revolutionary. Another ambitious project was the laying, in the early 1970s, of an interconnecting 42 inch main between the north and south of the Company area. This took eighteen months to complete but was cheaper than building new service reservoirs, and during the drought of 1976, millions of gallons of water from the Severn were pumped all the way from Hampton Loade up to Burton-on-Trent.

Today South Staffordshire Water supplies water to almost 600 square miles of the heart of England, from the fringe of the Peak District in the North to Halesowen in the south, from Kinver in the west to Burton-on-Trent in the east. It is proud of its 146 year history, during which time it has expanded and adapted, sometimes using pioneering engineering techniques, to meet the changing requirements of domestic and industrial customers. The story does not end here, however.

The company is leaner, fitter and more efficient than at any time in its history. By using modern management techniques and all the aids offered by science and technology it is well poised to meet all the challenges of the years to come.

The author and publishers are indebted to Johann Van-Leerzem and Brian Williams (both retired) from South Staffordshire Water PLC. Much of this text is based on their tireless research.

Top left: Wood Green re-pumping station.
Top right: The Triple Expansion Rotative Pumping Engine which replaced the Cornish Beam Engine.
Below: The result of a damaged water main on Wednesbury Road, New Mills, Walsall on 25th April, 1955.

Walsall College of Arts & Technology

The nineteenth century was a great period for self improvement when working men and women, often aided by local beneficiaries, established Mechanics Institutes and Reading Rooms. These were sometimes partly funded by local employers who appreciated the self-help example set by workers who paid their weekly penny subscriptions. Walsall was no exception, indeed the Mechanics Institute in Freer Street, founded in 1830 to improve the skills and moral character of mechanics, was one of the earliest in the Midlands.

From this simple beginning grew the present College of Arts and Technology. By 1854, the year the Crimean War started, the Walsall School of Design and Ornamental Art was founded by Mr W Smith, a local sculptor. Six years later he founded the Walsall Working Men's College. The descendants of the 'rude mechanicals' referred to by Shakespeare had got the bit between their teeth in this part of the West Midlands, then a geographic description rather than a planner's administrative dream, as The Walsall Science and Art Institute was formed in 1872.

French workers and intellectuals were then fighting in a bloody defence of the Paris 'Commune', following the collapse of the Second Napoleonic Empire to the Prussian onslaught. The working men and women of Walsall had sound realistic notions of

their route to success via the classes in Technical Education and other subjects offered by their local institute. This, too, grew as a result of its success and in 1908 moved to new, larger premises where it became the Walsall Institute of Art, one of many such educational establishments fostered in the halcyon pre-war days of Edwardian England.

During the 'War to end War' of 1914-1918 the Institute taught women and disabled soldiers side by side in the technical and other skills required for the home front. The year 1915 saw the Institute renamed, yet again, as Walsall Technical College in recognition of its purpose. During the inter-war years plans were made for new buildings to be erected in what had been the slums of Wisemore. Due to the recession of the 1930s and the pressures

Above: Motor vehicle students in the 1950s.
Below left: The final moments of the exam, 1953.
Below: Students relax before class.

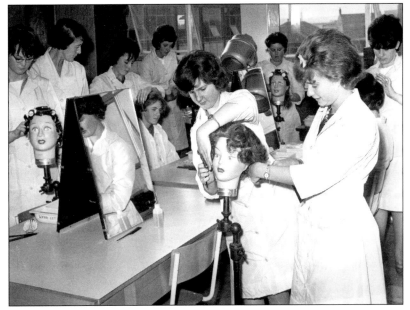

Nursing Course was launched in response to the Government White Paper 'Framework for Expansion'.

The need for training and upskilling in the 1980s led to further additions to the college with a new Business Studies Block and an additional Heavy Goods Vehicle Workshop in 1982. Now there were greater opportunities for the community to participate in training and education, and on 1st April 1993 the college became incorporated and merged with the former College of Art in Walsall at that time.

Walsall College of Arts & Technology continues to meet the demands of students internationally and has developed links throughout the world, including Europe, America, the Far East and Africa. The explosion of technology and the Super-highway with the rapid increase of Information Technology equipment and software has culminated in the building of the state-of-the-art European Design Centre.

of the 1939-1945 War, work was delayed until the heady days of the 1950s, exemplified by the Festival of Britain which heralded the 'New Elizabethan Age'.

The expansion of buildings to house departments old and new commenced, in 1952, with, appropriately enough, the Workshop block designed by Hickton, Madeley and Salt, architects. By the mid 50s the Laboratories and Drawing Office of the second phase were completed. Further additions were ready in time for the official opening ceremony by Professor Coulson, FRS on 18th October 1968. It was not part of the college's tradition to stand still and continuing expansion of courses and student numbers cried out for yet more accommodation. This demand was met, first in 1968 by the handsome Tower Block and later by space for the growing library facilities.

In the 1970s there were rapid changes in the educational and training sector. The college's reaction to these changes was pro-active and led to the expansion of Vocational Training. In 1974, following Local Government re-organisation the college was renamed Walsall College of Technology, a new Child Study Department opened and a two year Nursery

Built in 1997, the European Design Centre, partly funded by the European Regional Development Fund, houses the most up to date technology and was opened by Margaret Hodge MP on 5th February 1998. With this prestigious development, the college continues to push forward the boundaries of Education and Training into the next millennium, to create a Learning Borough offering lifelong learning for all.

Top left: *Hairdressing students in the 1960s.* *Above right: The college pictured in 1962.* *Left: Catering students pictured in the 1950s.* *Right: A night time view of the college in the 1990s.*

Fitted to perfection

Like many other people in the town of Walsall, Richard Taylor had become involved in the local trade, training in his younger years as a saddle tree maker. In the early 1920s he made what was destined to be a key career move, and took his craft a stage further. Working from a wooden building in his garden in Bath Road, he set up in business in 1923, using his skills to produce wooden prostheses - vital replacement body parts, while his wife Lilian carefully stitched together the necessary leather fitments and helped with the office work. In 1930 Mr Taylor's son Norman (currently the company's chairman) joined his parents in the business on a part time basis, moving into full time employment in 1948.

In those early days all the products were individually made by hand from materials such as wood, leather and steel, and only basic hand tools were used - a far cry from today's modern machinery! Plastics were in time introduced into the manufacturing process as well as MDF and stainless steel,

and the firm's wider range of up-to-date machinery includes lathes, routers, a wide range of drilling and cutting tools and welding and brazing equipment. The company expanded rapidly and began to produce surgical appliances (orthotics), eventually ceasing to produce artificial limbs.

In response to the expanding needs of the company a move was made in 1951 to a small manufacturing unit in Bath Road; a second move followed in 1957 to the firm's present site in Woodwards Road which itself was extended four times between 1965 and 1981.

A family firm in the true tradition, four generations of the family have been involved with R Taylor & Son. When the National Health Service was formed, Mr Norman Taylor moved to expand the company, establishing fitting clinics within many hospitals throughout the Midlands and Mid Wales, measuring and fitting the orthotic products. His wife Kathleen, who sadly died in the mid-1990s, also worked with the company. In 1965 Norman and Kathleen's son Michael - who is the present Managing Director - joined the family firm, continuing to develop the orthoptic services. He formed the Therapy Division in 1986.

Top left: *R H Taylor, founder of the company.*
Above centre: *The Woodwards Road premises.*
Right: *The plastic moulding department.*
Below: *Skilled technician using traditional methods of manufacture.*

Michael Taylor's wife Barbara, who is today the Company Secretary, started work with the firm in 1984. Michael and Barbara's daughter, Mrs Sarah Cullingworth, joined the company in 1990 as a Sales Executive, promoting and expanding the therapy side of the business.

Difficulties and challenges have been part and parcel of R Taylor & Sons' development. During World War II, for example, the firm had little opportunity for expansion and found themselves marking time. In such a specialised industry, finding skilled labour has been virtually impossible and technicians have always needed special training to meet the company's skill requirements, while orthotists have been trained in measuring and fitting to match the needs of each individual client. The increasing monetary restrictions placed on all NHS and Social Services have brought their own particular difficulties.

Having successfully overcome each problem as it arose, R Taylor & Sons have expanded with the years to supply orthotic products and therapy and rehabilitation equipment to a wide range of services,

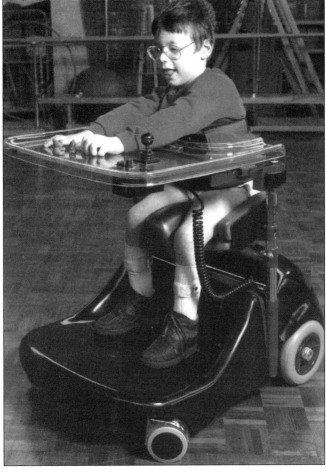

including the NHS, Social Services, Education Departments and Special Schools around Britain as well as to agents in Spain, France, Germany, Norway, Switzerland and Korea. In 1961 the company began to manufacture orthopaedic footwear - another interesting challenge.

Michael Taylor sees the company's desire to develop new and innovative products and concepts that meet the requirements of the individual as playing a key role in the firm's development. Modern technology has been introduced into the design process, and the in-house design team can be justifiably proud of the unique products they create with the aid of CAD CAM programmes.

The year 1998 was a jubilee year for Taylors, and the commemorative labels on their products read '75 years of care'. The company looks to the future years with hope that further generations of the family, having the same commitment to quality, service and value for money, will follow on to become involved in the long-established family firm.

Above: S.A.M. (Seating and Mobility System) - one of the new Therapy Products. Left: A view of the footwear manufacturing department. Below: N H Taylor, current Chairman of the company.

Beautiful leathers for a lifetime's pleasure - Whitehouse Cox and Company Ltd

Walsall has been famous since Mediaeval times for harness and leathergoods. The once prolific oakwoods of the Midlands provided the tannin to cure the skins of cattle and other beasts and to produce the fine English bridle leather for which Walsall is renowned. So it was, in 1870, when the horse was still king of the short distance transport world, Mr Samuel Cox and Mr Whitehouse set up in partnership to cater for the enormous trade in manufacturing leather harness.

Initially Whitehouse, Cox and Company continued as 'loriners' at Butts Road, casting the small metal buckles, clasps and hooks in steel and brass without which English harness cannot function. From here it was a logical step to making complete sets of 'tack' and building a reputation for fine workmanship recognised throughout the equestrian world.

The Company began to manufacture the many different designs of harness needed for draught horses of all sizes working on farms or drawing carriages and pony carts, drays and floats. Whitehouse Cox and Company began to make specialist goods such as saddles, bridles and martingales for hacks, hunters and military chargers, for which there was a constant demand. The quality of their crafts-manship encouraged a discerning and wealthy clientele who came, then as now, from all over England and parts of Europe for their saddlery and riding equipment.

In 1881 the partners made their second move, when Henry Cox built the new factory in Marsh Street which is still the company's home. The military requirements for tack and leather equipment of the South African War were but a prelude to the enormous market of the Great War.

Above: Mrs Edith Alice Cox pictured in her office in 1915. *Below:* The small foundry in Marsh Street where bits and stirrups were made.

leather briefcases. Collar and stud boxes are still made but are often adapted to ladies' use as jewellery boxes. More specifically Whitehouse Cox design and make ladies' hand bags, purses and tote bags in an exciting variety of leathers of different weights, textures and colours to suit the fashion needs of the occasion. Our flexible plastic friend has not been neglected as the range includes credit card holders to complement the wallets and handbags.

The snorting, explosive horseless carriage, initially the toy of the ultra-wealthy, heralded a new world which has virtually swept the horse from our streets and farms. The Cox family wisely saw the need to establish new markets for their skilled leatherworkers' products. Hard-wearing pigskin and distinctive crocodile skin for example have long been popular for luggage and small personal items such as shoes, purses and wallets. A glove factory was taken over and the company also started making leads and dog collars. The techniques and skills used in creating workaday harness were transferred to catering for much the same clientele living in the different world of the '30s and '40s.

The second world war, in spite of the use of canvas webbing, still created an enormous demand for leather war material both for personnel and for equipment of all sizes. Since then Whitehouse Cox have maintained their lead in producing fine leathers for those who not only enjoy the smell and feel of good skins but who appreciate well-designed goods which give a lifetime's use and value. Rare qualities these days!

The company's products are sold from their factory shop and throughout the UK, both in small independent retailers and in famous London department stores, wherever discerning people buy for themselves, their families and friends. The major export markets are Japan and the USA where shoppers go crazy over the English style to buy individual craftsmanship made to last in a world where built-in obsolescence is common.

Top left: Small leathergoods cutting department.
Top right: Warehouse and packing department.
Below: A selection of fine contemporary leather gifts, just some of the many lines created at Whitehouse Cox & Co Ltd, Crown Works, Marsh Street, Walsall.

For the dog in your life the company makes a hand-made range of plain and coloured, slim and sturdy collars and leads to suit the size of dog. Skirts and trousers can be matched by belts for every occasion in embossed or hand-plaited leather or genuine bridle leather coupled with buckles which reflect Whitehouse Cox's origins as loriner. Travellers will find the 'Pusser's Grip' style of light weight leather bound, zipped canvas bags provides decades of hardy wear whatever their mode of transport.

The gift range builds on an established tradition for gentlemen's wash and dressing kits, wallets, brush sets and key fobs and bridle

A century of leather curing expertise

James and Emmanuel Sedgwick founded their curriers business in 1900, in premises in Eldon Street, Walsall. Walsall has centuries of history in the production of leather and saddlery dependent on tanners who tan the raw hides and curriers who prepare the tanned hides for the leather workers. It is the curriers who process tanned hides from beef producing animals, so that they are ready for the equally diverse requirements of harness

and baggage makers, shoe makers, bridle and saddle makers and those making even softer and more flexible leather clothing.

Following the establishment of their business at their first premises the two Sedgwicks took into partnership Richard Farrow whose family still control the company. Like other firms in the leather trade Sedgwicks prospered due to the enormous demand for leather harness and equipment made by the exigencies of the Great War. Post war changes were brought about by the slow replacement throughout Britain, of horse drawn vehicles by motor transport. Farmers, hard hit by the Depression, continued to use horses

into the 1940s, and even later on a smaller scale. In the 1930s the company moved to a five storey building in Rushall Street where processing the tanned hides continued in time-honoured fashion. Currying was then largely a hand operation entirely dependent on skills of hand and eye developed by years of experience. Then as now Sedgwicks worked with ox hides, primarily from the meat industry which are rather sturdier and have a better grain quality than those of dairy breeds.

After the founders and Richard Farrow died Sedgwicks was run by the four sons of Richard Farrow working together in equal harness. During World War II the three younger brothers were called up into the armed forces. E H Farrow was left in charge to cope with wartime shortages of manpower and materials rationed out by the Ministry of Supply to suit the paramount needs of the 'war effort'. The war years were very difficult as were the post war years when heavy industry was given priority to rebuild Britain's export trade.

By 1954, only three years after the showcase Festival of Britain, and one year into the joyfully heralded New Elizabethan Age,

Above: The staff photographed in 1926.
Left: The premises on Rushall Street to where the company moved in 1929.
Below: A staff picture from 1935. The two Farrow brothers are seated in the centre of the bottom row.

Sedgwicks were confident enough of their place in a market wanting traditional crafts- manship and quality to move into their present premises at Reservoir Place in Pleck. No fear of the old Black Country joke about the unemployed 'missuring the raz with a pace o' twine' to occupy idle days here. Idle days are unknown in a company where skills honed by experience are extended by modern equipment to increase output for expanding markets at home and abroad. Tanning takes approximately six weeks before the hides are delivered to the curriers. Following a rigorous inspection the accepted hides are cut into the pieces required which are stamped with job numbers to identify source, work to be done and ultimately the customer. After soaking, the leather is split and shaved to the customer's thickness.

Iron stains left by different operations are cleaned by a further two days of vatting in Shumac,

which prepares the leather for re- tanning and dyeing. After drying and 'samm setting' the leather is oiled with cod oil to protect it while drying. The moisture content is reduced and it is then conditioned for hand setting. After the flesh side has been treated it is hung to dry for several days. Further inspections and gradings are made of the leather ready for buffing on the outer grain side and fluffing on the inner flesh side prior to staining and waxing dependent on its final use. After even more drying the leather is waxed with a mixture of tallow and oils, piled for a few days and then brushed before despatch to the customers.

Sedgwicks sell their cured hides to leather workers throughout the UK, Europe, North America, Australia, India and the Far East. The majority of these clients cater for those who prefer British workmanship aided by modern technology to their home cured products.

Top left: The second stage of the current premises at Reservoir Place, Pleck under construction in 1964.
Top right: Showing buffing operation in the first phase of the current premises in the late 50s.
Above right: The premises pictured shortly after completion in 1954.
Left: The Finishing shop in the late 50s.

This Company has got packaging taped

Castle Packaging Limited has been distributing tapes and packaging products from Walsall for 40 years; and if that seems impressive, compare it to its subsidiary Haynes of Leicester, which has distributed 3M products over 100 years. Then add it all together, and it comes to almost a century and a half - and that's a lot of 3M tape!

A disused chapel in Bott Lane, Walsall was Castle Packaging's elegant first home; Mr A E Dean and Mr B Castle first set up in business there as part of the Deanson Printing Group in 1957.

The new enterprise's major activity at first was the sale of gummed paper tape, evolving into self-adhesive tapes as technology improved and new products became available. The growing business remained in the Bott Lane chapel until

1963, when more room was required, and it then moved across the road into new, purpose-built premises. Further expansion took place in 1975, bringing the site up to its present 12000 square feet. In 1982 Castle Packaging Limited became independent from the Deanson Group; since that time growth has accelerated and the company has recently acquired the long-established G F Haynes Ltd of Leicester and Nottingham.

The packaging industry is intensely competitive, but by providing a high-quality service and a pro-active response to customer needs Castle Packaging has succeeded in establishing itself as one of the country's leading distributors of tapes and adhesives. They also supply a diverse range of standard and specialist packaging items. Their customer base spans all industries which use packaging, but is dominated by the sign, display, print and point-of-sale markets. Castle

Top right: The current premises undergoing gradual expansion during the 1970s. Left: The original premises pictured in 1957.

compliant computer system installed in November 1998. Plans for the future are, simply, to continue to grow at both the Walsall and the Leicester and Nottingham sites, and to expand through acquisition if suitable opportunities arise. Above all, Castle Packaging Limited will continue to maintain the high standards of service which it has set for itself, putting its customers first and helping them find the right solutions at the right time, for the right price.

Above left: The premises as they appear today.
Below: 3M, VHB tape etc being used to bond acrylic sheeting to aluminium in the construction of illuminated signs.

Packaging's trained sales personnel works closely with suppliers and customers to acquire both a detailed product knowledge and an in-depth understanding of what its customers do. This means that it is able to match the products available from innovative suppliers to the requirements of its customers.

Packaging is an industry which thrives on innovation, and therefore 'ideas selling' and the ability to identify new applications for products are important skills. Using suppliers who include 3M, Tesanet, Technibond, Permabond and Jiffy, Castle Packaging can employ its expertise, its experience and its contacts within the industry to source and supply any available product and even to have items 'tailor made' to an individual customer's specification, thus effectively providing a 'one-stop shop' for all its clients' tapes, adhesives and packaging needs.

In addition to helping its customers find the right products for their purposes, Castle Packaging places an equally high priority on ensuring a swift delivery. The trade counter is open all day, from 8.15am to 5pm, and a same-day local delivery service or 24 hour national delivery is offered on a comprehensive range of stock items.

The company attributes its growth and success in this competitive area to team efforts in maintaining consistently high levels of service and in offering quality products at a competitive price. It has a loyal staff of around 20, many of whom have served the company for a long time. Castle Packaging provides a high level of staff training, which includes organising Demonstration Workshops; these fulfill the dual functions of training staff and increasing customer awareness of new products. The company achieved the ISO 9002 standard via BSI in 1993, and is now ready for the new millennium, having had a new, Year 2000-

Are you sitting comfortably? Aulton & Butler Ltd's customers are...

In 1955 Jack Aulton and Dennis Butler set up in business in Milton Street, Walsall, equipped with bench drillers, a circular saw and a forge, and started making saddle trees. A saddle tree is the frame for a riding saddle. Mr Aulton was a woodworker by trade, and Mr Butler was a metalworker, and besides possessing all the requisite skills between them they also brought to the business many years' experience, having both been engaged in this type of work since the 1930's. The two men worked from their original premises in Milton Street for four years, and then moved to Shaw Street, where they remained for seven years. They next moved to Holly Hedge Lane, and eight years later they moved to their current premises at Ashtree Works at Bentley Lane, where the firm is now run by the second generation.

In spite of the name 'Ashtree Works', the principal material which the firm uses for its saddle trees these days is in fact birch. When Jack Aulton and Dennis Butler first started the business, they used hand-carved beech wood and hand-forged steel. Now, pressed steel is used instead of hand-forged steel, and laminated birch plywood has replaced beech, but the manufacturing process has remained essentially the same. Some saddle trees these days are made from synthetic materials, but Aulton and Butler use only wood. The use of wood allows them to work with a high degree of adaptability, and the firm can make saddle trees of all sizes, to fit anything from a Shetland pony to the largest heavyweight hunter.

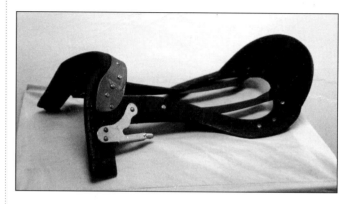

The saddle trees made at Ashtree Works are mostly destined for Walsall saddlemakers, although some are exported to Europe. At the saddlemakers, the trees are built into saddles for the leisure market, and there is no indication on the finished saddle as to where its tree was made, so unfortunately the firm has no way of knowing the end destination of its products. All that can be said is that there is a good chance that a comfortable saddle bought in the Walsall area has inside it an Aulton and Butler saddle tree.

Top left: Dennis Butler, one of the company's founders. Above: A finished saddle tree. Left: Jack Aulton, one of the company's founders. Below: The company premises today.

A family firm - built on success

The five divisions of the Kendrick Construction Group have grown from a modest family concern, founded in 1880 by Black Country bricklayer William Kendrick.

He had been working on the rapidly expanding streets then being built, prior to setting up as his own boss at what is still the company's headquarters in Tasker Street.

The Kendrick business grew together with its reputation, which even in the early days was recognised and perceived as a high quality local firm.

The Kendrick business developed with the growing importance of the Black Country. The individual nailers' and chain-maker businesses gave way to the large concerns that made the region synonymous with iron and steel.

Kendricks then and now supply the demand for industrial, corporate, commercial, healthcare, educational and leisure buildings, together with undertaking residential property development. Repairs and maintenance to buildings of all ages and types is the other major area of business activity, which still forms a vital part of the Group's activities.

During the second world war the company collected debris from bombed buildings, and was involved in the monumental task of clearing devastated Coventry, so that vital war work could continue. Walsall, and other Black Country towns too, needed to replace destroyed buildings of all kinds as quickly as post war priorities and limited supplies permitted. Debris was recycled both for repair work and to eke out rationed materials in new buildings.

The great wave of development in the contemporary era of the 1950s and 1960s saw Kendricks working more and more with all the Local Authorities in the West Midlands, hospital boards

and private industry to meet the demand for new and larger facilities in an expanding economy. This was matched by the continuing need for Local Authority housing to replace time worn stock throughout the region.

As wealth and educational needs grew the Kendrick Group had firmly established itself as a major construction player for the region noted for exceptional quality. The Company undertook major hotel projects and education schemes for several universities to cater for a population with greater expectancies for both leisure and higher education.

One of the factors relating to the Group's success is its philosophy of caring for all employees amongst whom very long service is common.

With its exceptional workforce and a strong network of subcontractors, Kendricks have maintained their century year old reputation for high quality workmanship, which time and time again has led to enormous customer satisfaction.

Kendricks now enjoys immense financial stability, so hard to achieve and so easy to lose, which has kept the organisation to the fore.

Top left: William Kendrick who founded the company in 1880. *Above:* The prestigious Symphony Court development in the heart of Birmingham. *Below:* An aerial view of the redeveloped football ground, the Hawthorns, home to West Bromwich Albion F.C.

Creating equine costume jewellery

William Thacker established W Thacker and Sons in 1845. He was joined by his two sons Will and Ernest towards the end of the last century. Since then they have stamped out millions of ornamental mountings for horse furniture, as harness is known. In Thacker's first 60 years private gentlemen ordered such stampings decorated with family heraldry for their carriage horses. Cavalry regiments also decorated their chargers' harness with regimental badges rather than the general service motifs of industrialised wars.

Although the Great War saw increased business for suppliers of horse furniture the new industries at the fore during the second world war made quite different demands on Thacker's workforce. A number of the firm's most skilled men were drafted to the Spitfire factory at Castle Bromwich to utilise their metal working skills in producing 'chargers for the knights of the air'.

In 1933 Alfred Alcock, then the foreman, had joined with Ernest Thacker's daughter Lena to buy the company from the founders. She retired in 1962 and

Alfred's son Peter joined the business in 1963. This successful family business still operates from its original site at Fieldgate in New Street, Walsall.

Whatever the changes in customers and markets Thackers still produce their wide range of goods by hand, aided by simple effective machines whose basic designs have barely altered in a century and a half. While equipment has been updated the actual techniques and operations are virtually unchanged.

Today their catalogue lists hundreds of intricate decorative pieces to enhance the appearance of leather harness. These traditional geometric and animal head designs, some of which originated to protect horse and rider from witches' spells, are produced and finished by hand. Such ornaments are purchased for dogs and other pets as well as for horses great and small. Customers include Icelandic reindeer owners as well as horse riders from Scandinavia, Western Europe, North America and Australia.

Peter Alcock likens his family business, in which he is aided by daughter Susan, the Company Secretary, to a cottage industry. It is one in which their small team of skilled press operators and stampers, braziers and polishers enjoy being part of the Walsall tradition.

Above: Thacker's as it was circa 1850s.
Left: Hand-stamping harness decorations on the original stamp. Below: The premises as they appear today.

Kirkpatrick Ltd - I mac siccar (I make certain)

customers regard as a craft product as opposed to mass-produced material.

During the war the making of builders' ironmongery changed to making fittings for ammunition and storage boxes in their countless thousands.

Today the company are still in their original Frederick Street works and still employing loyal members of the same skilled families that have been there for as long as the Kirkpatricks. Their functional and decorative Gothic-style products are found on the doors and windows of pubs, colleges and handsome homes throughout the British Isles. The builders' ironmongery range that the company produces is exported to numerous countries around the globe and one of its main selling points is that it is made in England and even today it is still made by similar processes to the way it has always been made.

The ancient Scots motto of the Kirkpatricks is a guarantee of sound quality dating back through a century and a half of iron founding in Walsall. William, the young migrant from Kirkcudbrightshire, probably learnt his trade from his brothers Thomas and John who had settled locally some years before his arrival in 1832. William Kirkpatrick, when in his late thirties, set up on his own as an iron caster in 1855.

Although he produced the popular Gothic and Mediaeval styles of door furniture and other iron work so much a part of the Victorian decorative scene, his early years were a struggle. Eventually quality told and William Kirkpatrick found time for the church and public works that his Covenanting upbringing demanded. From the Walsall School Board in 1877 he became Councillor and, nine years later, Mayor of Walsall until his death in 1887.

Kirkpatricks are proud of their history and their family links, as the oldest manufacturer in the business selling the largest range of antique style builders ironmongery available.

Above: The staff pictured in the late 1920s.
Below: An aerial view of the premises pictured in the early 1930s.

Today the company he founded in a strange country sells goods that he would recognise to lands around the globe. The original Black Country iron foundries worked by families or other small teams have given way to modern workshops. The furnaces and annealing ovens were originally fired by coal and coke but nowadays are either oil-fired or electric. However, the traditional skills of the area still play a vital part in the production of what

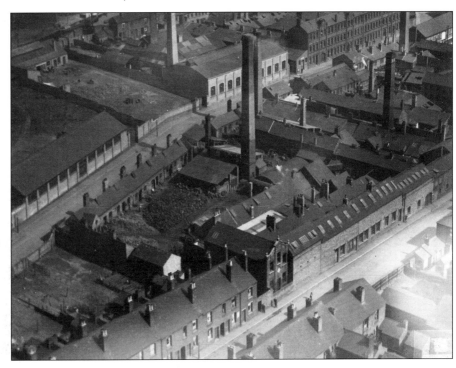

A man's job for good men

HP Westwood of Cheslyn Hay is the complete butcher who buys his stock on the hoof and slaughters it himself. As a lad Harold Westwood, the son of an insurance agent, spent his spare time helping at W Lockley's, the butchers in Bridgetown. By the age of ten he had killed and dressed his first sheep. (How many readers remember skinning a rabbit?) Basic equipment was the old-fashioned 'pole axe' for slaughtering and the wheel used to lift the half-ton or more carcasses to a convenient height for butchering.

In November 1937 he gave up his job at Taylor's Bakeries to take over a bankrupt butchery. He was helped first by his wife, Gladys, and later by their growing family. Shop facilities were much simpler then when many butchers without refrigerators sold off their stock on Saturday night at give-away prices.

During the war Gladys was left to do the demanding work with what help she could obtain while Harold was drafted into the National Fire Service, which was deemed more appropriate essential war work for a fit man than butchering. His worst memories are of the fire storms which raged through the naval depot and town of Plymouth during the worst of the 'Blitz'. Happier memories include the time a bull chased Harold around the yard before trotting back into its trailer.

Fans of the TV series 'Dad's Army' will have some idea of the difficulties of obtaining severely rationed meat supplies which made little allowance for the non-edible percentage of bone etc. Most people were glad to eat offal, an unloving term for delicious items such as chitterlings, sweetbreads, brains, liver and tripes.

Today the sparkling modernised shop and slaughterhouse is recognised by the Ministry of Agriculture. Beasts are felled by electric shock or stun gun and dressed under clinical conditions. Butchery is less physical than it was but the paper work has multiplied. Westwood have a fine reputation for preparing faggots, sausages, freezer joints and a good line of cooked meats, and are pleased to sell meat that always pleases the customer.

Above: Harold selecting the best sheep for his shop, 1959. Left: Harold and his wife serving customers with the finished product, 1959.

Bits, buckles and bells

Stanley Brothers Ltd started in Eldon Street in Walsall in 1832, five years before the young Queen Victoria ascended the throne. Throughout the great changes of her reign the horse remained king despite the advances of the steam railway system. Up-and-coming companies, such as Stanley Brothers, prospered by producing brass horse furnishings for leather tack.

All tradesmen's delivery vehicles were horse-drawn in an age when a smart turn-out was a vital advertising feature. Add to this the varied needs of the private carriage trade: all horsemasters required different sizes, shapes and qualities of buckles and bits appropriate to the occasion and value of horse or pony. Stanley Brothers catered for all types of equine establishment. The Army too had an insatiable appetite for tack as did the colonies still dependent on Home industries.

The Great War saw military demand for horse furniture escalate. The present owner's grandfather took control in the 1920s steering Stanley Brothers through the difficult years of the Depression. Farming was in such a pitiful state that few farmers bought new tack while many transport firms bought motor vehicles for speed and modernity. Landowners reduced the rising costs of their stables by buying motor cars. Stanley Brothers had to adapt to a rapidly changing world.

In 1935 the firm bought J Wedge and Son and moved into their larger premises in Intown Row, Walsall. A year later the current owner's father took over the enlarged company. During World War Two the unglamorous mule, using thousands of Stanley bits and buckles, was vital to carrying supplies, often airlifted, in Burma, the Balkans and the Italian Appennines. Since then Stanley Brothers have held their place in supplying top quality long-lasting bits, buckles and stirrups for the equestrian leisure market. Ornamental brasses are now sold as household ornaments rather than as the prizes and lucky charms of yesteryear.

The firm's major customers today are the saddlery wholesalers and the enormous variegated belt makers of the USA. In both these areas traditional British quality competes with the low labour costs of the Far East.

Top left: Examining a finished bit.
Top right: Adding the grip to the stirrup irons.
Left: Eric Bee Bee who ran the firm for 30 years.
Below: Pouring molten metal into moulds to create the quality bits, buckles and stirrups that Stanley Brothers are famous for.

The heavy rainstorm that turned Park Street into 'Park Lake' on 14th June 1931.

Acknowledgments

Walsall Local History Centre -
part of the Leisure and Community Services department of Walsall MBC

Liz Berry
Jack Haddock

Thanks are also due to:
Peggy Burns and Margaret Wakefield who penned the editorial text and
Mike Kirke for his copywriting skills